INTERNATIONAL RELATIONS IN ASIA, AFRICA AND THE AMERICAS

Edited by Andrzej Mania & Marcin Grabowski

VOL. 2

PETER LANG

A Short Guide to the New Silk Road

Adam Nobis

A Short Guide
to the New Silk Road

Translated by Patrycja Poniatowska

PETER LANG

Bibliographic Information published by the Deutsche Nationalbibliothek
The Deutsche Nationalbibliothek lists this publication in
the Deutsche Nationalbibliografie; detailed bibliographic
data is available in the internet at http://dnb.d-nb.de.

Library of Congress Cataloging-in-Publication Data
A CIP catalog record for this book has been applied for
at the Library of Congress.

Cover illustration: Courtesy of Benjamin Ben Chaim

ISSN 2511-588X
ISBN 978-3-631-74867-1 (Print)
E-ISBN 978-3-631-76046-8 (E-PDF)
E-ISBN 978-3-631-76047-5 (EPUB)
E-ISBN 978-3-631-76048-2 (MOBI)
DOI 10.3726/ b14324

© Peter Lang GmbH
Internationaler Verlag der Wissenschaften
Berlin 2018
All rights reserved.

Peter Lang – Berlin · Bern · Bruxelles · New York ·
Oxford · Warszawa · Wien

This publication has been peer reviewed.

www.peterlang.com

Introduction

Introduction

Many of us are well acquainted with the Silk Road. In recent years, however, a New Silk Road that has been on the lips of many. This short guide is addressed to all those who want to find out about this New Road in more detail. Like any short guide to a popular city, this guide offers only focuses on selected places, events and people and provides rather fragmentary information about them. Despite such limitations, this guide boasts a certain advantage. A monograph study of a city demands comprehensive descriptions and definitive conclusions. But what if we are dealing with a city which, though replete with various historic sights and monuments, is largely a construction site? Without offering a complete synthesis, this guide can help us move among such construction sites and compare an array of places with one another. Another advantage of this accessibly written guide is that it can be useful to very different people – students, entrepreneurs, scholars, tourists and all those who are curious about the world they live in. Its pocket size will not be a problem when we hit the road, no matter if we travel light, with a backpack or a briefcase. That it lacks conclusiveness and completeness is additionally motivated by the sheer volume and diversity of Silk Road plans and projects, most of which are developing as we speak (or read) of them and are modified in the process. To assess in how far this guide is helpful is up to its readers themselves.

The New Silk Road is a construction site. Some of its elements are ready, other ones are being constructed or designed, and still others will likely be devised in the future. Because I believe that this future is unforeseeable, I will not try and predict it. Instead, I will attempt to understand what is going on at this huge construction site – what is going on in the world we inhabit. Even this endeavour is thwarted somewhat by a very particular circumstance. Namely, various construction companies and teams are currently working there, and each of them implements its own projects and pursues its own aims. Their projects sometimes overlap and sometimes diverge conspicuously. The construction of the New Silk Road is an enterprise involving several countries, companies, organisations and individuals. This provokes inquiring whether there is one New Road or perhaps a multitude

of interrelated Roads. The latter was the case with the Silk Road which we are now bound to call "old" for the sake of clarity. I do not think this guide will answer this question for us. But I hope that the readers who look for answers to this and related questions, will find this guide helpful.

Now a short guide to this short guide. Like the Old Road, the New Road is a network of connections among various, distant places. Part 1 presents selected connections and places. Part 2 covers people, institutions and pro-jects, again not all of them, obviously. Part 3 lists meanings and values ascribed to the New Road by various people in various places. Part 4 offers a conclusion of sorts, against all odds and the reservations I articulated above. It defines what the New Road means to our world and its future. Like other guides, this one is not meant to be read page by page and entirely in one sitting. Rather, the readers are encouraged to find and read items of interest to them in the order of their own choosing.

1. Routes and places

1.1 Railways

1.1.1 Yiwu (义乌) – Madrid

On 18 November, 2014, the first direct freight train called Yixinou left Yiwu, east China, to arrive in Madrid 21 days later. The train consisted of 82 cars and its locomotives were changed every 800 kilometres. On 9 December, having travelled 13,052 kilometres, the train arrived at the Madrid Abroñigal station, where it was welcomed by Ana Pastor, Spain's Minister of Public Works and Transport. The train's route runs across China (Luoyang, Xian, Urumqi), Kazakhstan (Dostyk, Astana), Russia (Yekaterinburg, Moscow), Belarus (Brest), Poland (Warsaw), Germany (Berlin, Saarbrucken), France (Poitiers) and Spain (Irún). Underway, three boogie exchanges were necessary due to gauge differences: in Dostyk at the Chinese-Kazakh border, in Brest at the Belarussian-Polish border and, finally, in Irún at the French-Spanish border. The first cargo contained 1,400 tons of Christmas sale products. Having left Madrid on 29 January, the Yixinou returned to Yiwu on 22 February, carrying wine, olive, mineral water and Spanish ham.

Alexander, Harriet; World's
Burgen, Stephen; The Silk
Shepard, Wade; Why
Tharoor, Ishaan; The world's
Xie, Jun; Yiwu

1.1.2 Chengdu (成都) – Lodz

Since April 2013, freight trains from Chengdu, central China, have been coming to Lodz, Poland. The service is operated by Lodz-based Hatrans, which offers weekly express transport by 41 cars, reaching the destination within 14 days and crossing Kazakhstan, Russia and Belarus. The 9,826-kilometre-long route runs through China's Urumqi, Kazakhstan's Dostyk, Russia's Yekaterinburg and Moscow and Belarus's Brest. Initially, the cars came back empty. Only on 18 August, 2015, the first 42-car trainset loaded with 1,000 tons of coconut cookies, vodka, mineral water, beer and cider departed from the Lódź-Olechów station to Chengdu. Over the first two years, about 100 regular and 50 charter trains came from China, carrying textiles, electronic products, household utensils and car appliances. Going back, the trains carried Polish groceries.

Hatrans Logistics
Magnuszewska, Agnieszka; Łódź
Magnuszewska, Agnieszka; Pociągi
Magnuszewska, Agnieszka; W kwietniu

1.1.3 Lodz – Xiamen (厦门)

In August 2015, Hatrans started a freight train service from Lodz to the port of Xiamen on the Chinese coast of the Taiwan Strait. On 26 August, the first train headed to Xiamen departed from the Łódź-Olechów station. The event was attended by the Mayor of Lodz Helena Zdanowska, the Lodz Province Marshall Witold Stępień and the Deputy Mayor of Xiamen Yunfeng Zheng.[1] 15 days later, the train's 40 cars filled with products of the Lodz region: candies, beer and cider arrived at their destination. The nearly 11,000-kilometre-long route runs across Belarus (Brest), Russia (Moscow), Kazakhstan (Dostyk) and China (Urumqi, Chengdu).

Bińczyk, Beata; Inauguracja
Jędrzejczak, Agnieszka; Pierwszy

1.1.4 Zhengzhou (郑州) – Hamburg

DB Schenker launched a train service between Hamburg, Germany, and Zhengzhou, China. First, in August 2013, trains from China started to arrive in Germany, and on 1 September, 2014, the first train departed in the opposite direction. Besides representatives of the company and the municipality, among those gathered to festively wave the train good-bye was Fuzhan Xie, Governor of the Henan Province. The 10,214-kilometer-long route of the 41-cargo-container trainset ran through Germany (Duisburg), Poland (Warsaw, Małaszowice), Belarus (Brest, Minsk), Russia (Moscow),

---

1 Regardless of their respective nationalities, the various individuals in this guide are referred to by their first name followed by the surname. In the bibliography, they are listed alphabetically by their surnames, with the first names following after a comma.

Kazakhstan (Astana, Zharyk, Dostyk) and China (Urumqi). In 2015, trains left for China twice a month and to Germany twice a week. The trip took 16 to 18 days. Electronic and automotive goods travelled to Hamburg while the first train to China carried industrial automatic machines for technology companies.

DB Schenker; DB Schenker
Geodis; Eurasia
Good Hope Logistics; Freight
King, Mike; DB Schenker

1.1.5 Yiwu (义乌) – London

On 18 January, 2017, a train from Yiwu, east China, reached the cargo station of Barking in east London after 16 days of travel. Called the "East Wind," the train consisted of 34 cars carrying 68 containers with four million pounds' worth of cargo: clothes, suitcases, handbags and purses. In this way, a regular, weekly service between London and Yiwu was started with the aim to assess the demand. The train covered 11,999 kilometres across Kazakhstan, Russia, Belarus, Poland, Germany, Belgium and France to reach London via the Channel Tunnel. Patrick Sawer believes that the train's name is a reference to Chairman Mao's declaration that "The east wind will prevail over the west wind." He adds also that the event "signalled a new chapter in the history of the centuries-old trading route."[2]

Sawer, Patrick; East

1.1.6 Yiwu (义乌) – Tehran (تهران)

On 23 January, 2016, Iran's president Hassan Rouhani and China's President Jinping Xi met in Teheran to sign a trading agreement aimed to increase the countries' trading exchange up to $600 billion within the coming decade. Three weeks later, on 16 February, the first freight train from China's Yiwu reached Teheran, having covered 10,400 kilometres across Kazakhstan, Uzbekistan and Turkmenistan in 14 days. Its route ran through Chinese Urumqi, Kazakh Alma Ata, Kyrgyz Bishkek, Uzbek Tashkent and Samarkand, and Turkmen Ashgabat. The Russian news agency Sputnik

---

2   All the quotations are given with their original spelling, grammar and word-use.

announced the opening of a new service within the "Silk Road Economic Belt,"[3] and Director of Iran's national railways Mohsen Pour Seyed Aghaei told the Iranian agency Mehr that "countries along the Silk Road are striving to revive the ancient network of trade routes."

Cole, Juan; The Chinese
Dehghan, Saeed; China's
Sputnik; Historic

1.1.7 Moscow (Москва) – Beijing (北京)

British company Golden Eagle Luxury Trains offers Silk Road tourist trips by luxury trains from Moscow to Beijing, calling at Volgograd, Karakum Desert, Khiva, Ashgabat, Merv, Bukhara, Samarkand, Tashkent, Alma Ata, Turpan, Dunhuang and Xian. The trips involve also sightseeing in towns which were once crucial to the old Silk Road.

Golden Eagle Luxury Trains

1.1.8 Trans-American railway

During his visit to Latin America in the summer of 2014, President of the People's Republic of China Jinping Xi proposed his country's participation in the construction of a trans-American railroad connecting the continent's Pacific and Atlantic coasts. When China's Prime Minister Keigen Li came to South America, he met with President of Peru Ollant Humal on 19 May, 2015, and with President of Brazil Dilma Rousseff three days later. In both meetings, joint declarations were adopted to analyse the feasibility of the projected railway connection. On this occasion, Dilma Rousseff called the rail project put forward by China relevant to Brazil's development, and Ollant Humal described China's participation in its execution as necessary. The construction cost of a 5,300-kilometre-long railroad was estimated at $10 billion. In one of the plans, the route stretched from, in the west, the Peruvian port of Puerto Ilo, to Arequipa, Puno and Cusco, to Brazil's Madre de Dios, Rio Branco, Porto Velho, Vilhena, Cerrado Savana and Campinorte, to, finally, Porto do Açu on the Atlantic in the east.

---

3   Chinese documents define the project as "One Belt, One Road" (一带一路;) or, more concisely, as "Belt and Road."

Bazo, Mariana; China
Bland, Daniel; China
Diálogo Chino; The Transcontinental
Lee, Brianna; China
Nogaj, Wioletta; Kolejny

1.1.9 Trans-Siberian railway

The Trans-Siberian Railway connects Russia's European part to the Far East. 9,288-kilometre-long, the railroad's main route from Moscow to Vladivostok is the world's longest train route. Its construction started in 1891 and finished in 1904. The first station is Moscow's Yaroslavskaya station, followed by Yaroslavl, Kirov, Perm, Yekaterinburg, Tyumen, Omsk, Novosibirsk, Krasnoyarsk, Irkutsk, Ulan-Ude, Chita, Skovorodino, Khabarovsk and Ussuriysk, with the terminus in Vladivostok. The train passes through 87 cities and crosses 16 big rivers. The entire journey takes 6 to 7 days. The main route branches off into subsidiary ones. One of them is the trans-Manchurian line, which swerves off the main one at Chita and runs through Zabaykalsk, Qiqihar, Harbin, Changchun and Shenyang to Beijing. The Trans-Siberian railway serves both passenger and cargo transportation, facilitating transport across Russia between ports on the Pacific and ports on the Baltic and Black Seas. Passengers can use both luxury and common trains. Interestingly, the luxury train fares approximate flight prices.

RussiaPl.Info; Kolej
Транссибирская магистраль

1.1.10 Tashkent – Samarkand

In August 2011, the Uzbek national railways started a high-speed service from the capital city of Tashkent to Samarkand. Produced in Spain, the train covers the 344-kilometres-long distance within 2 hours and 10 minutes, morning and evening daily, with the maximum speed reaching 254 km/h. The train is called Afrasjab, after Samarkand's ancient name. In August 2015, the line was extended to Qarshi, and in August 2016, to Bukhara. The first travellers on board the train form Tashkent to Samarkand were the state dignitaries and foreign guests. Chris Moss wrote: "Samarkand's Registan (old town) remains the most evocative and exotic-looking city on the Silk

Road." Samarkand and Bukhara are inscribed in UNESCO's World Heritage List. The new line was constructed in order to boost tourism in the region.

Advantour
Atlanta Travel; New
dziennik.pl; Uzbecka
East Time; Uzbekistan
Moss, Chris; Silk

1.1.11 Tazara railway

The Tazara Railway is a 1,860-kilometre-long railroad of 1,076 mm track gauge, connecting Kapiri Mposhi in central Zambia's Copperbelt to Tanzania's port of Dar es Salaam on the Indian Ocean. It was constructed in 1970-1975 and financed by the People's Republic of China as the first Chinese investment of this scale outside China. It is operated by the Tanzania-Zambia Railway Authority (TAZARA). Often called Uhuru, which stands for "freedom" in Swahili, the railway was turned into a symbol of pan-African socialism by the Zambian and Tanzanian politicians of the day. In 2011, the Chinese government waived 50% of the debt incurred in constructing the line, and in 2014 representatives of China, Tanzania and Zambia decided to recapitalise the company.

Xinhua; Tazara

1.1.12 Nairobi – Mombasa

A planned railroad connecting Kenia's Nairobi to the port of Mombasa on the Indian Ocean (see Nairobi).

1.1.13 Angola's railways

3 separate railroads dating back to the colonial times. They lead to from Atlantic ports eastward to the continent's interior. The Northern line, called Luanda, connects Luanda to Malanje (424 km); the Central line, called Benguela, runs from Lobito to Lunau on the border with Zaire (1,344 km), where it joins the Katanga Railway going to Zaire's and Zambia's Copperbelt; and the Southern line, called Moçâmedes, connects Namibe and Menougue (860 km). The two former lines were modernised in 2006–2014 by China's national Railway Construction Corporation Ltd. with the participation of

100,00 Angolan workers. The opening ceremony of the modernised Benguela Line held in Luau on 14 February, 2015, was attended by the Presidents of Angola, Zaire and Zambia. The third line was modernised in 2006–2015 by the China Hyway Group, a Hong Kong-based private company.

Macau Hub; China
Railway Gazette; Three

1.1.14 Argentina's railways

During the visit of President of Argentina Cristina Fernández in Beijing on 13 July, 2010, a package of contracts was signed concerning the participation of Chinese companies in the construction and modernisation of railways in Argentina, funded by the China Development Bank. The contracts stipulate, for example, the provision of engines and cars of the Belgrano Argentinian national railways. Other items include the modernisation of the route from the river port of Timbúes on the southern Parana River, in the province of Santa Fe, to the northern cities of Salta in the Andes and Barranqueras on the Parana River at the border with Paraguay (1,500 km); the modernisation of the line from Buenos Aires to Mendoza in the west of the country; and the construction of 18 kilometres of the underground with 29 stations in Córdoba, extension of the Buenos Aires underground by a line to the Ezeiza airport and the provision of engines and cars for the underground trains. Chinese companies – the Beijing-based CITIC Group Corporation and the Xi'an-based Shaanxi Coal Group Investment Co Ltd. and China Railway First Survey & Design Institute Group Co Ltd. – are collaborating on the project.

Railway Gazette; China

1.1.15 New Amber Road

Rail Freight Corridor No. 5 – RFC5 – is a freight rail connection between the Baltic Sea and the Adriatic seaports, cutting through Poland, the Czech Republic, Slovakia, Austria, Slovenia and Italy. Designed by the European Commission and started in 2015, the connection has come to be called the New Amber Road. Radosław Pyffel explains that, in Poland, it is supposed to intersect with the China-envisioned East-West New Silk Road. The official website of RFC5 features a map showing a network linking the seaports of Świnoujście and Gdansk, via Wroclaw and Katowice in Poland, Czech Břeclav, Slovak Zilina and Bratislava, and Vienna to the seaports in Italy (Venice, Trieste and Ravenna) and Slovenia (Koper).

Na kolei; Nowy
Pyffel, Radosław; Nowy Jedwabny
RFC5 Baltic-Adriatic Corridor

1.2 Roads, bridges and tunnels

1.2.1 Karakoram highway

On 30 June, 2006, China's Assets Supervision and Administration Commission and Pakistan's National Highway Authority signed an agreement on the modernisation of the existing road and the construction of a new, 1,300-kilometre-long highway between Chinese Kashgar and Pakistani Abbottabad. The China Road & Bridge Corporation completed its work in September 2015. Cutting across the Karakoram Mountains from the east to the west via the Khunjerab Pass (Chinese: 红其拉甫山口, Urdu: درّہ خنجراب) on the China-Pakistan border at the altitude of 4,693m, it is one of the highest-situated highways in the world. The Karakoram Highway has contributed to reinvigorating vehicle traffic between Pakistan and China. It is highly relevant to the projects of connecting China's Kashgar to Pakistan's seaport of Gwadar. It promotes tourism in the region, which was once an area of early Chinese expeditions (e.g. of Faxian, a Buddhist monk, at the turn of the 4th century) and is now famous for its wealth of ancient and early medieval Silk Road monuments, among them images of Buddha carved on a rock in Skardu (Urdu: اسکردو).

Hodge, Adam; Karakoram
Sen, Tansen; The Travel

1.2.2 Bridge on the Panj River

26 August, 2007, saw an opening ceremony of a new bridge on the Panj River (Tajik: Панч), a subsidiary of the Amu Darya marking the border between Afghanistan and Tajikistan. The bridge connects the Afghan town of Sher Khan Bandar with Tajik Dosti. The event was attended by the Presidents of Afghanistan and Tajikistan: respectively, Hamid Karzai

and Emomali Rakhmon, and US Secretary of Trade Carlos Gutierrez. The 672-kilometre-long bridge was financed by the US and constructed by the Italian company Rizzani de Eccher. Emomali Rakhmon said: "The opening of this bridge provides a chance for boosting trade not only with Central Asian countries, but also with China, Russia and the Gulf countries."

BBC News; US

1.2.3 India-Afghanistan-Iran highway network

Iran, India and Afghanistan's collaborative project aims to develop and extend the countries' highway network. The project's important part is the construction of a highway connecting Iran's seaport and city of Chabahar with Afghanistan's cities of Zaranj and Delaram, where the planned highway is supposed to join the Afghan Herat-Kandahar highway. Indian minister Sushma Swaraj, who visited Iran on 16 April, 2016, said that the road would "facilitate the linking of Afghanistan and Central Asia with India." Saumya Sil added that, going through Iran's Chabahar, the road would "give India sea-land access to Afghanistan bypassing Pakistan." The construction of the Afghan part of the highway in 2009 was financed by India's government.

Devirupa, Mitra; With Chabahar
Sil, Saumya; Is Iran's

Talmiz, Ahmad; Who's

1.2.4 Marmaray tunnel

The 13.6-kilometre-long rail tunnel under the Bosphorus Strait (with the deepest part at 60.5 metres below the sea surface) connects the European and Asian parts of the Turkish railway grid as well as the European and Asian parts of Istanbul. The construction work started in 2004, and the tunnel was opened on 29 October, 2013. On the eve of the opening ceremony, Minister of Culture and Tourism of the Republic of Turkey Omer Celik said at the International Silk Road Congress in Istanbul: "The opening of the Marmaray Tunnel will bring about an uninterrupted and efficient functioning of the Silk Road as a route of transportation and exchange between East and West. Thus, the Marmaray Tunnel will be a strategic axis allowing the

Silk Road to regain its historical importance." And Binali Yildrim assured: "This project is not Turkey's project. This project is the project of the Silk Road which has been serving humanity for centuries and links Asia to Europe. This is a project which brings civilizations together. The Silk Road in not a caravan but rather a route linking western and eastern civilizations to one another." The tunnel facilitates national and international passenger and cargo rail transport. Participating in the opening ceremony of the tunnel at the Üsküdar Marmaray station in Istanbul's Asian part, Prime Minister of Turkey Recep Tayyip Erdogan described the tunnel as a part of the "Iron Silk Road" and added that, owing to the tunnel, which integrates railway networks of Asia and Europe, "We are connecting London to Beijing."

Daily News; Marmaray
Railway Gazette; Marmaray
Seibert, Thomas; Turkey
Turksoy; The Conference

1.3 By rail and by sea

On 31 January, 2016, a freight train carrying 20 containers from Ukraine reached China on what can be described as a test trip. The cargo left Ukraine's seaport of Chornomorsk near Odessa on a ferry on 15 January and, via the Black Sea, arrived in Georgia's Batumi, whence it travelled by train to Alyat, Azerbaijan. By ferry again, it reached Kazakhstan's seaport and city of Aktau and, again by train, via Jezkazgan and Dostyk, it crossed the Chinese border, having covered 5,471 kilometres. Three rail companies signed an agreement establishing the International Trans-Caspian Transport Consortium. The companies are: the ADY Express Ltd. and Logistics in Azerbaijan, the KTZ Express in Kazakhstan and the Trans Caucasus Terminals in Georgia, which decided to collaborate on developing cargo rail transport to and from China, Ukraine, Europe and Turkey, becoming in this way an important goods trade intermediary between the East and the West.

Babayeva, Fatma; Azerbaijan
Putz, Catherine; Why
Rutz, Julia; First
Shirinov, Rashid; Azerbaijan
Xinhua; Feature
Əliyeva, Aynur; Second

1.4 By sea

1.4.1 Shanghai – Hamburg

Shanghai is the world's biggest transhipment port while Hamburg is the second biggest port in Europe. Transport between the two ports is highly relevant to Europe's contacts with China. Founded in 2007, Shanghai Chin Young International Transportation Co., Ltd. offers "best freight rate from Shanghai to Hamburg." On its maiden voyage, the CSCL GLOBE, the world's biggest container ship (capacity: 19100 TEU;[4] length: 400 m; width: 59 m), called at the port of Hamburg on 16 January, 2015, and unloaded and loaded a total of about 11,000 TEU. Managing Director of China Shipping Agency (Germany) GmbH Niels Harnack said: "During the next few years we are reckoning with ongoing growth on the East Asia-Europe trade route and want to further expand our market share on this rotation. The Port of Hamburg plays a crucial part in this as a cargo source and transhipment hub – currently we are in Hamburg every week with seven services." The CSCL GLOBE gives Hamburg a connection with Shanghai and other Chinese ports: Tianjin, Qingdao, Ningbo, Nansha, Yantian. The ship is owned by the Shanghai-based China Shipping Container lines, part of the COSCO group. During its first voyage, the ship set off from China's Yantian and via the Suez Canal reached Great Britain's Felixstowe on the North Sea, from where it sailed to Rotterdam in the Netherlands, Hamburg in German and Zeebrugge in Belgium.

JCtransnet; Best
Mirror; Bigger
Port of Hamburg; Gigantic

1.4.2 Qingdao – Ras Tanura

China is dependent of crude oil imports, 80% of which comes by sea mainly from Saudi Arabia, where Ras Tanura in the Persian Bay is the biggest port with a crude oil loading terminal. In China, the biggest port with an oil unloading terminal is Qingdao on the Yellow Sea. Qingdao is also home to a refinery

---

4   Twenty-foot equivalent unit, i.e. the cargo capacity corresponding to the volume of a 20-foot-long (6.1-metre-long) container.

of the imported raw material, half of which arrives from Saudi Arabia. On 14 June, 2008, the Saudi Press Agency announced that the tanker Xin An Yang carrying crude oil for the refinery of Chinese company Sinopec entered the port of Qingdao. Crude oil has ever since kept coming to Qingdao and other Chinese ports from that and other Persian Bay ports via the Strait of Malacca.

Saudi Press Agency; Tanker

1.5 Canals

1.5.1 Nicaragua Canal

In 2012, the Hong Kong Nicaragua Canal Development was founded as a Hong Kong-based private company. On 13 June, 2013, Nicaragua's National Assembly agreed to grant the company a concession to design, construct and manage the canal for the following 50 years. It is designed to be 173 kilometres long, 250–580 metres wide and 90 metres deep. With these parameters, the canal would be bigger from the Panama Canal and, thus, make the navigation of bigger ships possible. Estimated at about $50 billion, the construction is to be completed by 2020. The planned canal would stretch between the mouth of the Brito river on the Pacific coast in the west and the Mexican Bay via Nicaragua and, further, along the Tule and the Punta Gordas rivers.

BBC News; Nicaragua
Daley, Suzanne; Lost
Grieger, Gisela; Nicaragua
Hołdys, Andrzej; Kanał
La Gaceta; Managua

1.5.2 Suez Canal (قناة السويس)

Dug in 1859–1869 through the Isthmus of Suez, the canal in Egypt links the Mediterranean Sea to the Red Sea. The canal is property of the Egyptian state and, since 1956, has been operated by the state company Suez Canal Authority (SCA), headed by Admiral Mohab Mohamed Hussien Mameesh (as of 2017). The canal is 193 kilometres long and 24 metres deep, which makes it accessible to ships up to the capacity of 240,000 DWT. In January 2016, the canal was crossed by 1,424 ships, therein 467 container ships, 387 tankers and 214 bulk carriers. SCA states that the canal "provides the shortest maritime route between Europe and the lands lying around the Indian and western Pacific oceans. It is one of the world's most heavily used shipping lanes. The Suez Canal is one of the most important waterways in the world."

The Suez Canal Authority

1.6 Ports

1.6.1 Piraeus (Πειραιάς)

On 1 October, 2009, the Piraeus Container Terminal (PTC) obtained a 35-years concession to operate container terminals in the Greek seaport of Piraeus. The company is owned by the China Ocean Shipping Company (COSCO), the second biggest port operator in the world, owned, in turn, by the People's Republic of China. As a result of the investment, the transhipment capacity of the port increased from 685,000 in 2010 to 3 million containers in 2015. By 2020, the PTC plans to make Piraeus the biggest Mediterranean port in this respect. President of the PRC Jinping Xi declared that his country wanted to make Greece a key link between Europe and China within collaborative operations informed by the "Belt and Road" project. Barely a year later, on 8 April, 2015, a new contract was signed in Athens, based on which the COSCO bought 67% of the shares in the Piraeus Port for €368.5 million and pledged to invest a further €350 million euro in the port's development over the following ten year. Present at the signing of the contract, Prime Minister of Greece Aleksis Tsipras said: "I think this agreement will shorten even more the Silk Road that brings goods from China to the Mediterranean and central Europe." Professor of Economy Ioannis Tzoannos, in turn, remarked that Greece was becoming an important component of the Sea Silk Route, which promoted trade, cultural exchange and collaboration in a range of fields.

Alderman, Liz; Port
China COSCO
Hope, Kerin; Greece
Johnson, Keith; In Odyssey
Lolos, Marios; Spotlight
Piraeus Container Terminal
Stamouli, Nektaria; Greece

1.6.2 Gwadar (گوادر)

On 30 January, 2013, Pakistan's government approved the transaction in which China Overseas Ports (COP) took over from Singapore's PSA the management of the Gwadar Port on the Balochistan coast. COP is a branch of China Overseas Holdings Limited, registered in Hong Kong, which is itself a subsidiary of the China State Construction Engineering Corporation, i.e. a state-owned company of the PRC. Additionally, the Chinese have leased 2,000 acres of land for 43 years to set up a Free Economic Zone in Gwadar. The port and the Zone are to be part of the planned China-Pakistan Economic Corridor (CPEC), connecting Kashgar, west China, to the Arab Sea. Totalling at nearly $50 billion, other planned investments within the CPEC project include the construction of highways, railways, a pipeline, an electric power plant and power lines. According to COP President Baozhong Zhang, the port will be fully operational by the end of 2017.

China Overseas Holdings
China Overseas Ports Holding
Raza, Syed Irfan; China
Sherazi, Syed Zubair; Development

1.6.3 Doraleh

A multipurpose seaport to be built based on a governmental agreement between China and Djibouti. The port is to be located west to the currently operating container terminal on the African coast of the Indian Ocean, in the Gulf of Aden near the entry to the Bāb al-Mandeb Strait, which links the Ocean with the Red Sea and, via the Suez Canal, further on to the Mediterranean. Worth $590 million, the investment is to be co-funded by China Merchants Holding International. On 8 April, 2016, the Chinese Ministry of Defence announced that the construction of China's first naval base beyond Chinese borders in Doraleh had started. François Dubé observes that the enterprise is part of the Chinese strategy of building "the 21st-century Maritime Silk Road" and quotes Weijian Li: "The facilities in Djibouti serve to protect China's economic interests in Africa and to help safeguard regional peace." Publishing satellite images of the construction in progress, Simon Tomlinson writes about the piracy-haunted Horn of Africa and adds: "The naval outpost, which is due for completion next year, is expected to feature weapons stores, ship and helicopter maintenance facilities and possibly special forces."

Dubé, François; China's
Tomlinson, Simon; China

1.7 Airports

1.7.1 Koktokay (可可托海)

On 1 August, 2015, the new Koktokay Airport was opened in the foothills of the Altai Mountains in the northern part of China's Xinjiang Uyghur Autonomous Region. The airport reduces the time it takes to travel to Urumqi, 400 kilometres away, from seven hours by land to merely 50 minutes of flight. In the first half of 2015, the Region was visited by nearly 16 million tourists from the PRC and over 667,000 travellers from abroad. According to the government's *China Daily*, the daily flight connections boost tourism and, consequently, the region's economic development by facilitating access for and, as a result, increasing the influx of Chinese and international tourists. The first plane had on board over 100 passengers, who, on landing, were given welcome by women wearing traditional Kazakh folk costumes. The government's information agencies advertise the Koktokay National Geopark as "an ideal place for sightseeing, vacationing, hiking, photographing and scientific expedition." The China National Tourist Office emphasises also that the entire region is a tourist attraction in itself as the historic Silk Road ran across it.

China Daily; Xinjiang
CNTO, Silk Road
People.cn; Xinjiang's

1.7.2 Dubai (دبي)

Sheikh Ahmed bin Saeed Al Maktoum called the Dubai Airport under his management the very heart of the New Silk Road. The Australian CEO of the Etihad Airlines, the United Arab Emirates' national carrier, James Hogan gives his airlines the very name of the New Silk Road. The Dubai Airport is one of the world's biggest international airports. In 2015, it handled 78 million passengers and 2.5 million tons of cargo, on 7,700 flights a week headed to 270 destinations in 6 continents and operated by 140 flight companies. The new airborne Silk Road seems genuinely global, which of course does not erase its specific locatedness in the city of Dubai on the Persian Gulf in the Emirate of Dubai, part of the United Arab Emirates.

Dubai Airports
Morgan Philips; Aviation
The Economist; Rulers
Topham, Gwyn; Emirates

1.8 Pipelines

1.8.1 TAPI pipeline

On 24 April, 2008, in Pakistan's capital Islamabad, an agreement was signed on the purchase of natural gas from Turkmenistan by Pakistan, Afghanistan and India. On 11 December, 2010, in Turkmenistan's capital Ashgabat, an intergovernmental agreement was signed on the construction of a pipeline to transport gas from the Turkmen gas deposits. In 2011, the project of the TAPI pipeline (Turkmenistan-Afghanistan-Pakistan-India) received support from US Secretary of State Hillary Clinton, who proposed a plan called "the New Silk Road," focused on the post-war reconstruction of Afghanistan. Due to be completed in December 2019, the project is to be implemented by state-owned Türkmengaz in collaboration with a consortium of Turkish and Japanese companies. On 13 December, 2015, the construction works were ceremonially commenced near Mara (ancient Merv) in the Karakum Desert, in the vicinity of the large Galkynysh gas field. It is here that the 1,814-kilometres-long pipeline is supposed to begin. The ceremony was attended by President of Turkmenistan Kurbanguly Berdymukhamedov, Prime Minister of Pakistan Nawaz Sharif, Vice-President of India Hamid Ansari and President of Afghanistan Ashraf Ghani, who referred to the project as "the New Silk Road." The pipeline is designed to run form the Turkmen Galkynysh field across Afghanistan, along the Herat-Kandahar highway, and further on near Pakistan's cities of Quetta and Multan, to terminate in the border town of Fazika, India.

Davis, Jonathan; Trio
Fedorenko, Vladimir; The New
Gurt, Marat; Olzhas Auyezov; Katya Golubkova; Jane Merriman; Turkmenistan
Reyaz M.; TAPI
Rubin, Barnett; The TAPI

1.8.2 Kazakhstan-China oil pipeline

In 1997, China and Kazakhstan signed an agreement on the construction of an oil pipeline. On 11 July, 2006, Kazakh oil reached China's border city of Alashankou on the Altai mountain pass Dzungarian Gate. In this way, the yet-uncompleted pipeline started to operate. The pipeline is owned jointly by the China National Petroleum Corporation and the Kazakh state-owned KazMunayGas. As of 2017, the pipeline is about 3,000 kilometres long and runs eastward from the Kazakh port of Atyrau on the Caspian Sea via Kenkiyak, Kumkol and Atasu to Alashankou in the Xinjiang Uyghur Autonomous Region. Branching off south- and northwards, it is connected with other pipelines, making up a grid linking Kazakhstan, Turkmenistan, Uzbekistan and China, whose total length exceeds 7,500 kilometres. This is the first land connection that permits oil supplies from Central Asia to China. Yin Juntai of the China Petroleum Exploration and Development Company observed that it reduced Chinese recipients' dependence on maritime oil shipments via the Malacca Strait, which had added up to 80% of China's oil imports.

> Lin, Christiana; The New
> Kosolapova, Elena; Kazakhstan
> Rakhmetova, Klara; Kazakhstan
> Rehn, Cecilia; Kazakhstan
> ҚазМұнайГаз; Kazakhstan

1.8.3 Turkish stream

On 1 December, 2014, Presidents of Russia and Turkey, Vladimir Putin and Recep Tayyit Erdogan, signed a preliminary agreement on the construction of a new natural gas pipeline across the bottom of the Black Sea. Gas is supposed to flow from the Anapa compressor station in Krasnodar Krai, Russia, to Kıyıköy in Turkey's European part, whence it is to be transported to Greece and other Euroepan countries. The investment is designed as a new element in the already operational Russian network transporting gas to Europe. Jean-Michel Valantin observes that it also entails increasing Turkey's significance as a transportation hub, which is, in turn, related to the Chinese initiative of "the New Silk Road." He writes also: "Beijing and Ankara are discussing the sino-turkish [sic] 'belt' of this 'new silk road,' called 'One Belt, One road,' or the 'Silk Road Economic Belt.'" Anna Keim and Sulmaan Khan, in turn, wonder: "Can China and Turkey forge a New Silk Road?"

Keim, Anna Beth; Sulmaan Khan; Can China
Valantin, Jean-Michel; Turkey: An Energy

1.8.4 Kunming-Kyaukphyu pipeline

On 29 January, 2015, a pipeline linking Burma's port of Kyaukphyu on the Indian Ocean to Kunming, the capital of the Chinese Junnan province, was put into service. It is parallel to a natural gas pipeline operational since 2013. Running across a challenging mountainous rainforest area, both pipelines help supply China with methane and crude oil from South Asia and the Near East, bypassing the Strait of Malacca. The project is a joint venture of companies based in China, India, South Korean and Myanmar (former Burma).

Meyer, Eric; With Oil

1.8.5 Baku-Tbilisi-Ceyhan oil pipeline (BTC)

Since July 2006, the Kazakh crude oil transported to the Azerbaijani port of Baku has flowed on through the pipeline to Turkish Ceyhan on the Mediterranean Sea and has been carried further on by sea to Europe. Leonard Coburn regards this and other pipelines as an important part of the New Silk Road.

Coburn, Leonard L.; Central Asia

1.9 Power lines and electric power plants

1.9.1 CASA-1000

Championed by the US diplomacy, the CASA-1000 project involves a high-voltage line supplying electric energy from hydro power plants of Tajikistan and Kyrgyzstan to Pakistan and Afghanistan. Worth nearly $1 billion, it is due to be completed by 2018. The project was developed in several meetings of Afghan, Kyrgyz, Pakistani, Tajik, World Bank, Islamic Development Bank, US and UK officials, held in such places as Alma Ata, Kazakhstan,

Guangzhou, China, and Istanbul, Turkey. The work commenced in May 2016. The plans include the construction of a power plant on the Vakhsh River near Nurek, Tajikistan, and a dam on the Naryn River near Toktogul in the Tian Shan Mountains, Kyrgyzstan. The power line running from the plant to the cities and towns of Pakistan and Afghanistan is to be connected with the already existing ones, such as the line from Uzbekistan's Termez to Afghanistan's Kabul and the line from the Tajik power plant of Sangtuda on the Vakhsh River to Pol-e Chomri, Afghanistan. These investments and connections can ultimately add up to an electric power grid covering entire Central and South Asia.

Casey, Michel; Investors
CASA 1000
Guzek, Paweł; Sangtuda
Fedorenko, Vladimir; The New
Trusewicz, Iwona; Prąd

1.9.2 Hydropower plants in Patagonia

A system of hydropower plants (Complejo hidroeléctrico Jorge Cepernic-Néstor Kirchner) with two dams on the Santa Cruz River in Patagonia, south Argentina. It was constructed upon a contract awarded to the Argentinian Mendoza-based company Electroingenieria e Hidrocuyo and the Chinese state-owned Gezhouba Group Company Ltd. of Wuhan in central China.

Watts, Jonathan; Argentina
Xinhua; Argentina

1.10 Telecommunications

1.10.1 Telecommunications in Africa

A mobile phone boom is sweeping across Africa. As Alfred Wong reports, the number of mobile phones in Africa leaped from 90 million in 2007 to 475 million in 2013 and is expected to increase further – up to 930 million by 2019. This development has been greatly boosted by Chinese telecommunications companies Huawei, Alcatel Shanghai Bell, China Mobile and ZTE. The companies operate particularly robustly in Algeria, Angola, Egypt, Morocco, Nigeria, Tunisia and the Republic of South Africa. The Chinese companies supply the equipment and become telecommunications network operators alone or in collaboration with local national firms and/ or international companies. The relevance of the telecommunications development to the New Silk Road is insightfully discussed by Gustavo Plácido Dos Santos.

Plácido Dos Santos, Gustavo; The United
Wong, Alfred; China's

1.10.2 Satellite communications

Estación del Espacio Lejano (China Satellite Launch and Tracking Control General CLTC). Approved by Argentina's Congress on 25 February, 2015, the Chinese ground-based satellite space station with a 35-metre-diameter antenna has been under construction in the surroundings of Las Lajas in the Argentinian province of Neuquén since 2013. Its main purposes include serving gorund communication but also tracking the planned Chinese missions to the Moon and Mars. The installation is scheduled to go into operation in March 2017.

Goñi, Uki; Argentinian
Lee, Victor Robert; China

1.11 Mines

1.11.1 Aktogay (Ақтоғай)

A copper mine in West Kazakhstan (250 kilometres away from the border with China), operated by the Kazakh firm KAZ Minerals funded from a China Development Bank loan of $4.2 billion. The international contract stipulates that copper extracted and purified at Aktogay is to be exported to China, the world's biggest copper importer. Molybdenum is to be a by-product of the mine's copper extraction.

Kaz Minerals, Aktogay
Mining Technology, Aktogay

1.11.2 Natalka (Наталка)

A gold mine at Kolyma, in Russia's Far East, 400 kilometres north of the Pacific port of Magadan. According to an agreement signed by the Russian firm Polyus Gold and the China National Gold Group Corporation, with

President Vladimir Putin and President Jinping Xi in attendance, Russia and China are to start digging gold together in 2017. The mine is to yield 15 tons of the metal yearly.

Polyus; Natalka
The Siberian Times; Major

1.11.3 Tenke Fungurume

A mine in the South-Eastern part of the Democratic Republic of Kongo. It has one of the world's largest deposits of copper and cobalt. The China Molybdenum Co. (CMOC) became the majority owner of the mine by purchasing its shares from the US-based Freeport-McMoRan's for $2.6 million. Discussing Chinese investments in copper excavation across the world, Dave Forest refers to them as a "Copper's New Silk Road."

Chan, Vinicy; Silk
Forest, Dave; Prime Meridians: A Journey
Pinto, Anet Josline; Denny Thomas; Freeport

1.11.4 Las Bambas

A mine in Apurímac, about 60 kilometres south-east of Cusco, Peru. In 2014, it was purchased from the Swiss Glencore for $5.85 billion by the Chinese company MMG Limited based in Melbourne, Australia. Andrew Michelmore expects the mine to be one of the world's most important copper mines by 2020. Its by-products are silver and gold.

Post, Colin; Las

1.12 Places

1.12.1 Aktau (Ақтау)

A seaport city on the Caspian Sea in Kazakhstan, with a population of about 150,000. An important hub of passenger and cargo shipping between the ports of Alyat (Azerbaijan), Atyrau (Kazakhstan), Türkmenbaşy (Turkmenistan), Rasht (Iran) and Astrakhan (Russia). It enables cargo to be transloaded from trains to ferries and the other way round, which facilitates transportation to and from China, on the one hand, and Azerbaijan,

Georgia, Iran and Turkey on the other. An excellent case in point is the Nomad Express running from Shihezi, China, via Dostyk, Kazakhstan, to Aktau, from where the cargo goes by ferry to Alyat, Azerbaijan and, transloaded onto trains, reaches Baku.

Gasimli, Vusal; The New
Kamalova, Gyuzel; Tatyana Kuzmina; New
Қазақстан темір жолы; Seaport

1.12.2 Alashankou (阿拉山口)

A Chinese town (40,000 population) in the Xinjiang Uyghur Autonomous Region located in the Altai's Dzungarian Gate (Chinese: 阿拉山口, Kazakh: Жетісу қақпасы), on the border with Kazakhstan. It is an important railway station for China's connections with the Caspian Sea countries and Europe and the place of boogie exchanges necessitated by gauge differences – in China and Europe 1,435 mm and in Kazakhstan and Russia 1,520 mm. On 23 December, 2009, a Free Trade Zone was opened here for the Kazakh citizens. The Dzungarian Gate has been used by the nomad peoples inhabiting Eurasian steppes for centuries. It was an important pass for the Silk Road. In the 2nd century B.C., it was crossed by Qian Zhang, an envoy of the Chinese Emperor Wudi of the Han dynasty, on a mission to the kingdoms of Central Asia.

Azaaroll, Augusto; An Early
China Knowlegde; The Shiji
Encyclopaedia Iranica; Chinese
HKTDC; What
KazWorldInfo; Trade Zone
Kouros, Alexis; The New

1.12.3 Alma Ata (Kazakh: Almaty, Russian: Алматы)

The biggest city of Kazakhstan (1.5 million population) and an international airport. It is situated in the foothills of the Tian Shan mountains in east Kazakhstan. On 25 November, 2015, the "Almaty Agreement" was signed here by Afghanistan, Bhutan, China, Iran, Kazakhstan, Kyrgyzstan, South Korea, Nepal, Pakistan, Tajikistan, Turkey, Turkmenistan, Uzbekistan and UNESCO. The Agreement concerns an international collaboration project aimed to preserve the Silk Road cultural heritage and to build on it in boosting tourism.

Almaty Agreement
New China; One
Winter, Tim; One

1.12.4 Alyat (Ələt)

A seaport town on the Caspian Sea in Azerbaijan (13,000 population). It is crucial to passenger and cargo sea traffic between the seaports of Azerbaijan, Kazakhstan, Turkmenistan, Iran and Russia and important to freight rail transportation between China and the Caspian Sea countries. Cargo is transloaded here from train cars to ferries, and the other way round. The port is central to the implementation of the Silk Road Project Azerbaijan funded by Saudi Arabia's Islamic Development Bank, part of the TRACECA programme (Transport Corridor Europe-Caucasus-Asia).

Gasimli, Vusal; The New
Gücüyener, Ayhan; Alyat
Islamic Development Bank; Aid

1.12.5 Astana (Астана)

The capital of Kazakhstan (over 800,000 population). It is an important railway station in linking China to the Caspian Sea countries and Europe as well as a popular conference and diplomatic talks venue relevant to the New Silk Road. On 7 September, 2013, at the local Nursultan Nazarbayev University, President of the People's Republic of China Jinping Xi gave a speech titled "Promote People-to-People Friendship and Create a Better Future," in which he described the Chinese ideas of building the Silk Road Economic Belt.

Dyussembekova, Zhazira; Silk
Ministry of Foreign Affairs of the People's Republic of China; President
Schaefer, Michael; Co-Driving
Turebekova, Aiman; Kazakhstan
Xi, Jinping; Speech at Nazarbayev

1.12.6 Baku (Bakı)

The capital and biggest city of Azerbaijan (2 million population). Dating back to at least the 12th century, it is the largest and oldest Caspian seaport. It plays an important role in communications among the Caspian Sea countries: Azerbaijan, Kazakhstan, Turkmenistan, Iran and Russia. It is also relevant to railway transportation between China and the Caucasus countries (Azerbaijan and Georgia) as well as to the planned trans-Caucasian train service to Turkey (from Baku via Georgia's Tbilisi and Achalkalaki to Turkey's Kars). On 25–27 April, 2016, the city hosted the 7th Global Forum of the United Nations Alliance of Civilizations convened under the theme *Living Together in Inclusive Societies.*

Azerbaijan; History
Forrest, Brett; The New
Global Forum Baku 2016
Rukhadze, Vasili; Completion

1.12.7 Beijing (北京)

The capital of the People's Republic of China and one of the world's largest cities (21 million population). It is an important railway node, operating train connections between Moscow and Hong Kong, as well as a nexus of expressways linking the city to the country's other regions. In 2015, the Beijing Capital International Airport served over 90 million passengers and handled over 1.8 million tons cargo on over 580 thousand flights. The city is the seat of the Asian Infrastructure Investment Bank (AIIB), established on 25 December, 2015, by the PRC and assembling fifty-seven countries from all over the world, as well as of several central state institutions, whose decisions determine several New Silk Road projects and enterprises. The Great Hall of the People located on the Tiananmen Square is the meeting place of the National People's Congress (全国人民代表大会), which, under China's current constitution, is the highest organ of state power. The Congress elects President of the People's Republic of China, the function now held by Jinping Xi (as of 2017). The Zhongnanhai building complex, which is part of the former Imperial City, is the main seat of the Communist Party of China.

Asian Infrastructure Investment Bank
News of the Communist Party
Beijing Capital International Airport
The National People's Congress
Trans-Siberian Travel

1.12.8 Belgrade (Београд)

The capital of Serbia (1.6 million population). On 16–17 December, 2014, the city hosted the 3rd Meeting of Heads of Government of China and Central and Eastern European Countries, attended by the Prime Ministers of China and 17 European countries (Albania, Bosnia and Herzegovina, Bulgaria, Croatia, the Czech Republic, Estonia, Hungary, Lithuania, Latvia, Macedonia, Montenegro, Poland, Romania, Serbia, Slovakia and Slovenia). Those gathered discussed possibilities of collaboration and exchange between China and Europe. The host of the meeting, Serbia's Prime Minister Aleksandar Vučić, said: "Serbia is regarded as the crossroads, where the economies, traffic and cultures of South-East Europe meet, and as the bridge connecting the East and the West of the 21st century." On 18 December, 2014, in the morning, Vučić and the Chinese Prime Minister Keqian Li officially opened a new bridge on the Danube constructed by the Chinese company China Road and Bridge Corporation. The bridge is meant to improve the railway connection between Europe's mainland and the Piraeus port operated by the Chinese COSCO.

Belgrade Meeting, Belgrade
Cooperation between China and Central
Serbia Construction; Chinese

1.12.9 Chengdu (成都)

A city in central China (4 million population) and a seat of the Sichuan provincial government. It is an important railway hub and a key station of Europe-bound freight trains as well as home to the busy international Chengdu Shuangliu Airport. Two thousand years ago, it was already an important trading centre of the Southern Silk Road, whose side-branches ran from China to Burma, India and Vietnam. The modern-day city is a remarkable tourist attraction offering Old Silk Road trips such as, for example, the "8 Days Silk Road Tour with Chengdu Panda" advertised by the Chengdu-based China Discovery. It is also highly attractive to foreign investors as suggested by the fact that 262 out of the Fortune Global 500 biggest companies do business in Chengdu.

China Discovery; 8 Days
HKTDT Research; The Belt
Hogg, Rachael; China
Kyle, Wang; Chengdu
Li, Yu; Chao Peng; Yining Peng; Chengdu
Travel Guide China; Southern Silk Road

1.12.10 Chongqing (重庆)

A city (4.8 million population) on the Yangtze in central China. On 13–15 October, 2016, the city hosted a conference of the Communist Party of China devoted to *The CPC in Dialogue with the World* and attended by over 300 participants from more than fifty countries. In his opening address, Yunshan Liu, a member of the Party's Political Bureau, said that the Party sought to develop collaboration with parties of other countries to streamline the management of the global economy. One of the focal themes of the meeting was the "One Belt, One Road" project.

China Daily, CPC
Wiadomości, Chiny

1.12.11 Chornomorsk (Чорноморськ)

A seaport city (70,000 population) on the Black Sea, 20 kilometres west of Odessa, Ukraine. An important link in freight transportation between China and Europe, where the cargo is transloaded from train cars to ferries and the other way round. In this way, the goods from China's Alashankou can get by rail to the Kazakh port of Aktau, from where they are carried by ferries across the Caspian Sea to Alyat, Azerbaijan and, on, by rail to Georgia's ports of Poti and Batumi. Further, the cargoes travel across the Black Sea to Chornomorsk, whence, loaded onto trains again, they are transported to Hungary, Slovakia, Belarus, Poland and Lithuania.

Centre for Transport Strategies; New
Kozak, Michał; Ukraine

1.12.12 Dostyk (Достык)

A Kazakh town in the Dzungarian Gate on the border with China. It is a railway station where boogie exchanges are performed due to the gauge difference between China (1,435 mm) and Kazakhstan (1,520 mm). Connected to Alashankou on the Chinese side of the Dzungarian Gate, Dostyk is instrumental to rail transportation between China, on the one hand, and the Caspian Sea countries and Europe, on the other.

Bradsher, Keith; Hauling
Chinese Turkestan
Nuttall, Clare; Building
Slobodchuk, Sergey; New

1.12.13 Dubai (دبي)

A city (2.6 million population) in the Persian Gulf, the capital of the Dubai Emirate, part of the United Arab Emirates. Its international seaport Jebel Ali is the world's ninth busiest transhipment port (about 14 mln TEU in 2013). Its international airport (see 1.7.2.) is also one of the biggest in the world. Its technological park Dubai Internet City includes Facebook, LinkedIn, Google, Dell, Intel, Huawei, Samsung, IBM, Oracle Corporation, Tata Consultancy, 3M, Sun Microsystems, Cisco, HP and Nokia. Sheikhh Nahyan bin Mubarak, Minister of Science of the United Arab Emirates, has observed that Dubai finds itself not only on the maritime Silk Road but also on the airborne and electronic Silk Roads. Dubai is a seat of many global financial companies, such as the New Silk Road Company LTD. Its Burj Khalifa (829 m) is the world's tallest structure, and the Dubai Mall, home to over 1,200 stores, is the world's largest shopping mall, which served 80 million customers in 2014. Dating back to the Bronze Age, the Iron Age and the Middle Ages, the archaeological sites in Dubai (Al Sufouh) and its vicinity (Al Ain in the Abu Zabi Emirate) as well as in other locations along the Gulf coastline (e.g. Bahrain) testify to a long-standing trading history of Dubai and its area. Already four thousand years ago, port settlements were set up on the coast where the Peninsula's overland caravan routes met with maritime routes. They were also intermediate stops in overseas commerce between the cities of Mesopotamia and the Gulf, on the one hand, and the countries of Africa, Asia and the Indian Ocean countries, such as Oman, on the other.

Dubai International Financial Centre
Kane, Frank; New Silk
UAE Interact; New archaeological discovery
The Dubai Mall
The National Council for Tourism

1.12.14 Duisburg

A German city (487 thousand population) on the Rhein in the state of North Rhein-Westphalia. One of the world's largest inland ports, it receives also sea ships although it is situated over 200 kilometres away from the coastline. The city is surrounded by six highways and is an important railway hub for the Zhengzhou-Hamburg railway and other trains to and from China. Already in the 9th and 10th centuries, Duisburg played an important role in trade contacts along the Rhein, bridging the North Sea and the Mediterranean Sea.

Chen, Xiangming; Julia Mardeusz; China
Forss, Pearl; Anthony Morse; China's
Fremde Impulse; The city
Makinen, Julie; Violet Law; China's

1.12.15 Guangzhou (Canton, Chinese: 广州)

A Chinese city (13 million population) in the delta of the Pearl River at its mouth to the South China Sea. It is a huge sea- and inland port with connections to over 300 ports in over 80 countries. Its international Baiyun Airport served 55 million passengers in 2015. The city is crucial to the Chinese "One Belt, One Road" strategy of the New Silk Road. It played a key role in China's maritime contacts with the world already in the early Middle Ages as a port attracting Persian and Arab merchants. Written records of Guangzhou can be found in *Information on China and India* by Sulaiman al-Tajir (Solomon the Merchant), a travel account authored around 851. The Hausheng mosque constructed under the Song Dynasty or the Tang Dynasty is also a testimony to the city's contacts with the Muslim world.

China Highlights; Maritime
The Danish Chamber of Commerce
Zaborski; Wspaniały Świat

1.12.16 Hamburg

A German city (1.8 million population) and a road and railway traffic hub. It is home to an international airport, the terminal of a railway line to Zhengzhou and other cities of China and a seaport on the Elbe. Located 110 kilometres away from the river's North Sea mouth, the port is Europe's second busiest ports (9.3 million TEU in 2013). Expanded in the 12th century, it was an important trading hub of the North Sea and the Baltic to grow even more in prominence as commerce with America across the Atlantic Ocean began.

FrankWaterloo; New
HKTDC Research; The Belt
Port of Hamburg; History

1.12.17 Herat (هرات)

A city in West Afghanistan (436,000 population) and the capital of the Herat province. Connected with Kandahar in the eastern part of the country, it is instrumental to transit traffic through Afghanistan. Since the Persian times, the city has been located at the intersection of routes leading northward to Merv and Bukhara, eastward to Balkh and China, southward to Kerman and Iran's other cities, and westward to Iran's Nishapur and, on, to Constantinople (later Istanbul). Included in the UNESCO World Heritage List, Herat is a popular tourist attraction advertised by travel agencies all over the world.

Harold, Frank; Herat
Kucera, Joshua; U.S.
UNESCO; The City
UNESCO Silk Road; Herat
Waugh, Daniel C.; The Silk

1.12.18 Hong Kong (香港)

A Chinese city (7.3 million population) and a Special Administration region of the People's Republic of China on the coast of the South China Sea. Its international airport served 68.5 million passengers in 2015, and its Stock Exchange ranks among the world's biggest. It has a robust seaport (transhipment of 2.3 mln TEU in 2014). The city is one of the pillars of the Chinese "21st-Century Maritime Silk Road" project aimed to increase and facilitate

China's contacts with South-Western Asia. On 18 May, 2016, Hong Kong
hosted an international conference devoted to the "Belt & Road."

Belt and Road Summit
Dworakowska, Katarzyna; Port
HKTDC; Belt
Lee, Eddie; Hong
Sant, Shannon Van; Hong

1.12.19 Istanbul (former Constantinople, Turkish: İstanbul)

Turkey's biggest city (14 million population) situated on both sides of the
Bosphorus Strait, which divides Europe and Asia. The Strait itself is a key
shipping lane connecting the Black Sea to the Sea of Marmara and, further,
the Aegean Sea and the Mediterranean. On 28–30 October, 2013, the International Silk Road Congress focused on *Rethinking the Road of Trade,
Cooperation and Peace* was held in Istanbul under the patronage of Turkey's President; the participants discussed "the need to revive the Historic
Silk Road." Turkey's biggest international airport – Atatürk Uluslararası
Havalimanı – is located in Istanbul's European part. The airport served 60
million passengers in 2015, as a result becoming the world's 10th and Europe's
3rd busiest airport (after London's Heathrow and Paris's Charles de Gaulle).
The city boasts a long and illustrious history: from a Bronze Age settlement,
to a Greek colony, a Roman city and the Byzantine capital, to the capital of
the Ottoman Empire after being captured by the Turks in 1453. Istanbul was
an important node of the old Silk Road, mediating the contacts between the
East and Europe. Key to this position were the city's maritime links to Venice.

Abu-Lughod, Janet; Before
INOMISC; International
Istanbul Ataturk Airport
Stahl, Alan; Zecca
Turksoy; The Conference

1.12.20 Jezkazgan (Kazakh: Жезқазған)

A city (100,000 population) in central Kazakhstan. It is a transit railway
station of the line connecting China with the Caspian Sea countries, Ukraine
and other European countries as well as of the line linking China to Poland,
Germany and other European countries via Russia and Belarus.

Acar, A. Zafer; Zbigniew Bentyn; Batuhan Kocaoğlu; Logistic
Chernov, Vitaly; Russia's
Daly, John C.K.; China

1.12.21 Kashgar (Chinese: 喀什, Uyghur: قەشقەر)

A city (340,000 population) in China's Xinjiang Uyghur Autonomous Region. Populated largely by the Muslim Uyghurs and boasting a large pigeon market, the city is highly relevant to the project of the China-Pakistan Economic Corridor connecting Kashgar with the Pakistani seaport of Gwadar. It was a very important place on the old Silk Road, with east to it, two routes bypassing the Taklamakan Desert – one in the north and the other in the south – and leading to Chinese cities. West of Kashgar, the roads branched off and led northward to Siberia, westward to Central Asia and southward to India.

BBC News; Is China
Gilad, Uri; Marika Vicziany; Xuan Zhu; At the
Kundu, Shohini; The New
Levin, Dan; Silk
Liu, Jing; The ancient

1.12.22 Lodz (Polish: Łódź)

A city in Central Poland (700 thousand population). It is an important road and railway traffic hub. In operation since 2013, the Lodz-Chengdu freight trains provide the first regular railway service from Poland to China. In 2015, a cargo line from Lodz to Xiamen on the Chinese coast of the Taiwan Strait was started. Both lines are operated by a Lodz-based company headed by Tomasz Grzelak.

Możdżyński, Bogdan; Chiński

1.12.23 Małaszewice

A small town in Poland (1,700 population) at the border with Belarus. Its international importance is founded on its frontier railway station, where the change of track gauges takes place as the former-USSR countries use the broad-gauge rolling stock (1,520 mm) while Poland and other European countries rely on the standard gauge (1,435 mm). It is an intermediate stop for trains connecting China to Lodz, Berlin, Saarbrucken, Madrid and other cities of Western Europe.

Hatrans Logistics; New

1.12.24 Minsk (Мінск)

The capital of Belarus (1.9 million population). Minsk is a station that serves trains travelling between China and Poland, Germany and other West-European countries. The 80-km^2 Great Stone China-Belarus Industrial Park is being developed 25 kilometres east of the city at the Berlin-Moscow M1 highway. Manufactured here, the produce of Chinese companies is to be sent to the European Union and the Commonwealth of Independent States. Commenced in 2012, the park's construction is due to be completed in 2042. 80% of the planned cost of $30 billion is to be financed by China. President of the People's Republic of China Jinping Xi called the investment "a pearl on the Silk Road economic initiative."

EuroBelarus; As
Gruszczyński, Bartosz; Chińskie
Xinhuanet; Xi's visit

1.12.25 Mombasa

A port city on the Indian Ocean in Kenya (1.2 million population). It has an ocean port, tanker loading terminals and container transhipment terminals for transloading. It has one of Africa's busiest container ports managed by the state-owned company Kenya Ports Authority. It plays a special role in the Chinese project of "The 21st-Century Maritime Silk Road" and features on its many maps. In the Middle Ages, it was one of the ports of the old maritime Silk Road, receiving ships from several ports of the Indian Ocean, India, Malaya and China.

Abu-Lughod, Janet; Before
Asante, Molefi Kete; The History
Moritz, Rudolf; One
The Maritime Executive; China

1.12.26 Nairobi

The capital of Kenya (3.4 million population). Its international Jomo Kenyatta Airport operates flights to over 50 countries in three continents of the Old World, with 19,000 passengers, on the average, checking in daily. Nairobi is the seat of the Sino Africa Centre of Excellence Foundation, whose "objective is to facilitate China-Africa trade and investment." Adedana Ashebir of the Foundation has told the Sputnik Agency that "Kenya will become Africa's gateway for business, investment and trade. One Belt, One Road policy is essentially creating a new maritime silk road... This will connect Europe, Asia and Africa through various ports. It will help Kenya become an even greater hub in the region for trade." On 12 May, 2014, a railway construction agreement was signed in Nairobi with Chinese Prime Minister Keqiang Li in attendance. Linking Nairobi to Mombasa, Kenya's port city on the Indian Ocean, the 610-kilometre-long line is to be co-funded by China and constructed by Chinese companies by 2018. It is planned to be extended to Uganda, Rwanda, Urundi and South Sudan in the future.

BBC News; China
Kenya Airports Authority; Nairobi
Levchenko, Anastasia; Kenya
Parke, Phoebe; Kenya's
SACE Foundation
Tiezzi, Shannon; China's

1.12.27 Porto do Açu

A seaport on the Atlantic Ocean in Sao Joao da Barra, Rio de Janeiro state, Brazil. In 2012, it was opened to China's huge container ships capable of transporting 400,000 tons of cargo. Speaking of it, Andrew Korybko stated: "The Silk Road stretches to South America." In China's project of the Trans-American Railway, Porto do Açu is to be connected by trains to Peru's Puerto Ilo on the Pacific.

Korybko, Andrew; China's
Phillips, Tom; Brazil's

1.12.28 Puerto Ilo

A Peruvian seaport on the Pacific Ocean. China's project of Trans-American Railway envisages connecting Puerto Ilo to Brazilian Porto do Açu on the Atlantic Ocean. Sylwester Szafarz discusses it in his "Stare i Nowe Szlaki Jedwabne" [Old and New Silk Roads].

Korybko, Andrew; The Silk
Municipalidad Provincial De Ilo
Szafarz, Sylwester; Stare

1.12.29 Shanghai (上海)

A Chinese port city (over 24 million population in 2015) on the South China Sea in the Yangtze River delta. It is the world's most populated city and busiest transhipment port (33.6 million TEU in 2013). Shanghai has been awarded a key position in China's maritime contacts within the "The 21st-Century Maritime Silk Road" project. It is home to the Shanghai Tower (632 m), the world's second tallest structure. On 14–15 June, 2001, the Shanghai Cooperation Organisation was established in Shanghai, and on 10–11 March, 2016, the city hosted the Global Conference on *Silk Road: Eurasia Connectivity,* in which Chinese and Italian politicians, scholars and entrepreneurs discussed the development of China-Italy relations.

BAA Global Conference
Shanghai Cooperation Organization
Shanghai International Port

1.12.30 Strait of Malacca (Selat Melaka)

A 36-kilometre-wide strait between the Malay Peninsula and the island of Sumatra, linking the Indian Ocean to the Pacific Ocean. It is one of the most important international shipping lanes, crucial to exports from China to Europe, South Asia, the Near East and Africa and to their imports of raw materials, food and other goods to China. Nearly 80% of crude oil imported in 2015 by China from Brazil, Venezuela, the US, Zaire, Angola, Saudi Arabia, Oman, Kuwait, Iraq and the United Arab Emirates arrived in China by tankers via the Strait of Malacca. One of the reasons behind Chinese proposal to build the New Silk Road is the striving to make China less dependent on this route.

A Crucial Feature
Clover, Charles; Lucy Hornby; China's
Cheng, Shuaihua; China's
QIC; The New
Wheeler, Andre; The New

1.12.31 Tashkent (Uzbek: Тошкент)

The capital of Uzbekistan (2.3 million population). Its international Toshkent Xalqaro Airport, one of Central Asia's important airports, served nearly 3 million passengers in 2014. The city is connected to Samarkand by a hig-speed rail line. On 23–24 June, 2016, heads of state of the Shanghai Cooperation Organisation countries met in Tashkent. Richard Covington calls Tashkent the "heart of the New Silk Road." Founded in Antiquity as an oasis in the western foothills of the Tian Shan Mountains, it is a very old city which was once an important hub of the old Silk Road, located at the intersection of various routes. One of them was an eastward route to the Fergana Valley. Another one headed south-west to Samarkand, where it branched off and led further southward to Bukhara and Mara (former Merv) and westward to Khiva. Yet another route went northward via Shymkent to South Siberia. Tashkent was mentioned in the *Great Tang Records on the Western Regions* (大唐西域記) by Chinese monk and traveller Xuanzang (玄奘), who visited the city in the 7th century.

Covington, Richard; Hearts
Uzbekistan Today; Tashkent

1.12.32 Torugart Pass (Chinese: 图噜噶尔特山口, Kyrgyz: Торугарт)

A pass in the Tian Shan Mountains near Chatyr-Kul Lake (Kyrgyz: Чатыркөл) at the altitude of 3,752 m. It is a border-crossing point between Kyrgyzstan and the People's Republic of China on the route leading from Kashgar in China's Xinjiang Uyghur Autonomous Region, northward by the international E125 road, to Kyrgyz Naryn (Kyrgyz: Нарын), Balykchy (Kyrgyz: Балыкчы) and Bishkek (Kyrgyz: Бишкек), Kyrgyzstan's capital. The route was once an important stretch of the Silk Road, with roads leading from Bishkek eastward to Alma Ata, westward to Central Asia and northward to Siberia. Today, the pass is a tourist attraction for travellers visiting the old Silk Road locations. It features, for example, in the itinerary of a trip offered by the US-based Silk Road Treasure Tours and advertised by the agency as the "Authentic Silk Road Journey of a Lifetime."

Caravanistan; Torugart
Азаттык; Торугарт

1.12.33 Urumqi (Chinese: 乌鲁木齐, Uyghur ﻧﯘﺭﯗﻣﭽﻰ)

A Chinese city (over 3 million population) and the capital of the Xinjiang Uyghur Autonomous Region. Its international Ürümqi-Diwopu Airport was used by over 18 million passengers in 2015. It is an important railway station of the line linking Yiwu, south China, to Europe and Teheran, Iran. On 23–25 July, 2015, it hosted the Silk Road Economic Belt Cities Cooperation and Development Forum, in which researchers, entrepreneurs and officials from 55 cities in 17 countries discussed collaboration in trade, industry and the Internet. In Chinese projects, the city is envisioned as an important tourist, trade and communication hub of the "Silk Road Economic Belt" initiative. It is home to the Xinjiang Silk Road Museum (新疆丝绸之路博物馆) and the International Grand Bazaar, one of the world's largest markets.

Cole, Juan; The Chinese
The Economic Times; 55 cities
Winter, Tim; One
Wu, Annie; Xinjiang
Wu, Annie; Urumqi

1.12.34 Venice (Italian: Venezia)

A seaport city on the Adriatic in south Italy (270 thousand population). It is represented in the maps of the New Silk Road published by the Chinese news agency Xinhua. It is the final port of destination of the Road's maritime part, which leads from Shanghai and China's other ports via the Strait of Malacca, India's Kolkata, Kenya's Nairobi, the Suez Canal and Greece's Piraeus, to Venice. Here starts the land stretch of the Road running along the Rhein to Dutch Rotterdam and, further, via Moscow and Central Asia, to Chinese Urumqi and other regions of China. Set up in the 5th century, the city took part in the old Silk Road transactions, mediating between Europe and countries of the East. In 1271, Marco Polo set off from Venice on his journey that took him to China to return to Venice in 1295.

Abu-Lughod, Janet; Before
Tiezzi, Shannon; China's

1.12.35 Xiamen (Amoy, Chinese: 厦门)

A port city (3.5 million population) on the Taiwan Strait in south-west China. Its international Xiamen Gaoqi Airport served 20.8 million passengers in 2015, and its ocean port, China's 8th busiest one, handles ships from over 50 countries from all over the world and ferries to Taiwan (8 million TEU in 2013). Ever since the early Middle Ages, the city has been important to China's maritime contacts with the world. Now, it has a relevant position in China's new strategy of "The 21st-Century Maritime Silk Road." It is the venue of the annual China International Fair for Investment and Trade. Antwerp-based Mathias Mertens wrote on visiting the city: "Today over 90% of trade between Europe and China travels by sea and the Silk Road has become the domain of archaeologists and historians. Nonetheless talk of a New Silk Road can be heard in all corners of the world."

Ge, Huang; Xiamen
Mertens, Matthias; Along
World Port Source; Port
Zhen, Luo; One

1.12.36 Xi'an (Chinese: 西安)

A city in central China (8.7 million population). A railway and road traffic node (3 highways), Xi'an has an express train connection to Zhengzhou and is an intermediary station of the Yiwu-Madrid line, the Chongqing-Duisburg line and other lines linking Chinese and European cities. The Xi'an Xianyang International Airport served nearly 33 million passengers in 2015. In 1991, the High-Tech Industrial Development Zone was established in Xi'an, comprising investments of over 1,200 international companies based in the Netherlands, Japan, South Korea, Germany and the US. Known as Chang'an in the past, it is one of China's oldest cities, the country's former capital under many dynasties and the beginning and end of many roads making up the Silk Road network. The tomb of China's first emperor Qin Shi, dating back to 210 B.C., and its world-famous terracotta army make Xi'an a very popular tourist attraction. Currently, according to the National Development and Reforms Commission, the city is to serve as the logistics hub for land and maritime links between Asia and Europe under The Silk Road Economic Belt project.

China; Xi'an
UNCTAD; Investment, s. 17
UNESCO; Xi'an
Wong, Tsoi-lai Catherine; Xi'an

1.12.37 Yekaterinburg (Russian: Екатеринбург)

A Russian city (1.4 million population) in the eastern foothills of the Urals. The city is an important railway hub, where the Moscow-Vladivostok Trans-Siberian Railway intersects with the routes of trains heading to China from Europe (e.g. from Lodz, Duisburg and Hamburg). Yekaterinburg was founded in 1723 on the Siberian route linking China to Russia via Irkutsk, Tomsk, Tobolsk, Yekaterinburg, Perm, Kazan and Moscow.

Engdahl, F. William; China's
Eurasian Business Briefing; New
Kolej Transsyberyjska; Jekaterynburg
Tian, Xuefei; All

1.12.38 Yiwu (Chinese: 义乌)

A city in east China (1.2 million population). A railway station and the terminal of international freight trains. The departure and destination station of trains to Madrid and other cities of Europe. It is home to the Yiwu International Trade Mart (the world's largest wholesale market complex) and over 70 thousand stores.

Huang, Flora; Yiwu
Yiwu Market Guide

1.12.39 Zhengzhou (Chinese: 郑州)

A city in east China (6.4 million population). It is an important railway hub and the departure station of three important westbound lines: via Urumqi, Alashankou, Astana, Oktyabrsk, Brest and Warsaw to Prague,

Duisburg, Hamburg, Paris and Milan; via China's Manzhouli, Russia's Novosibirsk, Yekaterinburg and Moscow, Belarus's Minsk and Brest, and Poland's Warsaw, on to West-European cities; and via Alashankou to Alma Ata in Kazakhstan. The international Zhengzhou Xinzheng Airport served 17.3 million passengers in 2015.

Aneja, Atul; Zhengzhou
Makinen, Julie; Violet Law; China's
Zhengzhou International Hub

2. People, institutions and projects

2.1 Asian Development Bank (ADB)

An international financial institution based in Mandaluyong, Philippines, founded in 1966. It assembles 67 members, thereof 48 from Asia and 19 from other continents, with the USA and the PRC among them. The Bank describes itself as "a financial institution that would be Asian in character and foster economic growth and cooperation in one of the poorest regions in the world." Under the motto of "The New Silk Road," it funds the Central Asia Regional Economic Cooperation Program focused on the cooperation in transportation and energy production among Afghanistan, Azerbaijan, the PRC, Kazakhstan, Kyrgyzstan, Mongolia, Pakistan, Tajikistan, Turkmenistan and Uzbekistan. It finances the TAPI gas pipeline projected to carry gas from Turkmenistan to Afghanistan, Pakistan and India (cf. 1.6.1).

Asian Development Bank
Asian Development Bank; The New

2.2 Asian Infrastructure Investment Bank (AIIB)

An international financial institutions based in Beijing, set up on the Chinese initiative as a result of a series of negotiations held in Kunming (PRC), Mumbai (India), Alma Ata (Kazakhstan) and Singapore in 2014–15. The agreement became effective on 25 December, 2015. The Bank assembles fifty-seven countries: Australia, Austria, Azerbaijan, Bangladesh, Brazil, Brunei, Burma, Cambodia, Denmark, Egypt, Finland, France, Georgia, Germany, Great Britain, Iceland, India, Indonesia, Iran, Israel, Italy, Jordan, Kazakhstan, Kuwait, Kyrgyzstan, Laos, Luxemburg, Malaysia, the Maldives, Malta, Mongolia, Nepal, the Netherlands, New Zealand, Norway, Oman, Pakistan, the Philippines, Poland, Portugal, the PRC, Qatar, the RSA, Russia, Saudi Arabia, Singapore, South Korea, Spain, Sri Lanka, Sweden, Switzerland, Tajikistan, Thailand, Turkey, the United Arab Emirates, Uzbekistan and Vietnam. The USA, Japan and Canada are the G7 major industrial nations which have not joined the Bank. Peimin Ni of the US writes that, unlike the World Bank and the International Monetary Fund, where the US has a veto right, the AIIB does not give a veto right even to its biggest shareholder, the PRC. He cites it as exemplifying the philosophy of "the new world order," which is to be polycentric and "not vertical, but horizontal," that is, founded on "dialogue, partnership, and cooperation" among countries, instead of on domination.

Asian Infrastructure Investment Bank
Ni, Peimin; The Underlying

2.3 Athens Silk Road International Travel

A travel agency "founded in Athens, Greece, on August 2000 by Mr. Lan Xiaocheng" to give Chinese and Greek tourists an opportunity to admire both countries' respective beauties and charms.

Silk Road International Travel

2.4 Bangladesh-China-India-Myanmar Economic Corridor (BCIM)

An international cooperation forum founded as a result of an agreement signed in Chinese Kunming, capital of the Junnan Province, in August 1999. It aims to strengthen trade, tourist and cultural ties and human contacts in the region and to construct and develop land roads, waterways, flight and telecommunication connections and pipelines between Kunming, China, and Kolkata, India, across Bangladesh and Myanmar (former Burma). The forum organises conferences, seminars and the BCIM car rally, which departed on 22 February, 2013, from Kolkata to Kunming along the nearly 3,000 kilometres of the planned investments.

BCIM Car Rally 2013
Institute of Chinese Studies; Bangladesh
Rupak, Bhattacharjee; The emerging

2.5 China Ocean Shipping Company (COSCO)

A Chinese state-owned maritime transport company. With the headquarters in Beijing, it has branches and subsidiaries in several countries across various continents, among them in Greek Piraeus (see 1.6.1.). It is one of the world's largest shipping operators, owning over 160 container ships with a total capacity in excess of 750,000 TEU. It boasts the biggest tanker fleet worldwide (in terms of both the number of ships and their capacity) as well as one of the world's largest bulk carrier fleet. Its ships enter over 1,000 ports in 6 continents.

China Ocean Shipping Company
Koutantou, Angeliki; Brenda Goh; After
Zhong, Nan; COSCO

2.6 Clinton, Hillary

US Secretary of State in 2009–13. On 20 July, 2011, in India's Chennai (former Madras), she said: "Historically, the nations of South and Central Asia were connected to each other and the rest of the continent by a sprawling trading network called the Silk Road. (…) Let's work together to create a new Silk Road." On her return from Asia in September 2011, she presented a project of Afghanistan's post-war reconstruction through developing the infrastructure linking the country to Central Asia, India and Pakistan. The project was labelled as the "New Silk Road Initiative." As Theresa Fallon writes, a Chinese diplomat described China's response to employing the term "Silk Road" in American policies in the following way: "When [the] U.S. initiated this we were devastated. We had long sleepless nights. And after two years, President Xi proposed [a] strategic vision of our new concept of Silk Road."

Clinton, Hillary Rodham; Remarks
Fallon, Theresa; The New
Fedorenko, Vladimir; The New
Kucera, Joshua; The New
U.S. Department of State; New

2.7 Communist Party of China (CPC) (中国共产党)

Founded in 1921, the governing party of the People's Republic of China with the central seat of power in Beijing. Its major organs are the National Congress and the Central Committee. In 2015, the CPC had 87.8 million members. Since 2012, Jinping Xi has been its General Secretary, combining this function with the position of President of the PRC. The party's decisions determine China's policies and politics. China's representative to the UN explains that new Chinese "Belt and Road" initiatives "have been written into the documents of the Third Plenum of the 18th CPC Central Committee." Jinping Xi's initiative has been presented and discussed in the party's several meetings and assemblies. For example, on 24–25 October, 2013, at the Peripheral Diplomacy Work Conference in Beijing, where the party's current foreign policy was planned, Xi said: "We should join hands with relative countries to accelerate infrastructure interconnection and intercommunication, and construct the 'Silk Road' economic belt and the '21st-Century Marine Silk Road.'" To enact the party's policy, its official newspaper, *People's Daily* (人民日报), has set up a special information platform devoted to the "New Silk Road" and "aiming at promoting the economic cooperation, culture exchanges, friendly relationships between China and other Silk Road countries."

Chinese Government, China Council
China Investments Research; Chinese
Mission of the People's Republic
News of The Communist Party
People's Daily; Of the

2.8 DB Schenker

An international German company with the headquarters in Berlin and over 2,000 agencies across the world. The company's mission is to "support industry and trade in the global exchange of goods through land transport, worldwide air and ocean freight, contract logistics and supply chain management." The company's Board of Management is chaired by Jochen Thewes (as of 2017). Under the "Modern Silk Road" offer, the company provides freight services between China's Shanghai and Germany's Hamburg: by sea (35–40 days), by rail (14–18 days) and by air (1 day). Its other railway services include the Suzhou (China) – Warsaw (Poland), Harbin (China) – Hamburg (Germany), Brest (Belarus) – Zabaykalsk (Russia), Wuhan (China) – Duisburg/Hamburg (Germany), Shenyang (China) – Leipzig (Germany), Chongqing (China) – Duisburg (Germany), Zhengzhou (China) – Hamburg (Germany) and Chengdu (China) – Lodz (Poland) lines. The company also offers complex shipment services between China and

Brazil, involving railway transportation from China to Germany and air transportation from Germany to Brazil.

DB Schenker
Wollmer, Göran; The Modern

2.9 Eurasian Economic Union (EAEU) (Евразийский экономический союз)

Established by a treaty signed in Astana, Kazakhstan's capital, on 29 May, 2014, by the Presidents of Russia, Kazakhstan and Belarus: Vladimir Putin, Nursultan Nazarbayev and Aleksandr Lukashenko, respectively. The preamble of the treaty defines the Union's fundamental pillars: the UN, the WTO, sovereignty and equality of states, human cooperation respecting histories, cultures and traditions, bilateral benefits, sustainable and fair trade and development and Eurasian economic integration. At a Kremlin meeting with President Jinping Xi on 8 May, 2015, Vladimir Putin said: "We think that the Eurasian integration project and the Silk Road Economic Belt project complement each other very harmoniously." Responding, Jinping Xi declared: "We agreed on the need to continue expanding our cooperation in various practical areas. We will give particular attention to finding common ground in China's development of the Silk Road Economic Belt, Russia's efforts to build Trans-Eurasian transport links, and the Eurasian Economic Union integration project. We will work towards greater mutual openness, coordinate our development strategies and deepen and interweave our interests for the good of both countries and peoples."

Eurasian Econiomic Union
Nazemroaya, Mahdi Darius; Neither
President of Russia; Press
President of Russia; Treaty

2.10 Ghani, Ashraf Ahmadzaj (Pashto: اشرف غني احمدزی)

President of the Islamic Republic of Afghanistan since 29 September, 2014. Proponent of the "Azure Route," the idea of which was presented, among others, during a visit in Azerbaijan in December 2014. According to Ashraf Ghani, "God willing, within three years from now, the Azure Route will link us to the continent of Europe via the Central Asian States and Turkey."

Zarghona Salehi adds that the road is to run "through Turkmenistan, Azerbaijan, Georgia and the Black Sea." Atiqullah Nasrat, Head of the Afghan Commerce and Industry Chamber, defined the Route's topography more accurately: from Afghanistan's Herat, via Turkmenistan's port of Türkmenbaşy on the Caspian Sea, and by sea to Azerbaijan's Baku. He emphasised also the Route's relevance to the region's development. Quoting President Khan Saif Shadi, he explained that "the route is named after a precious gemstone found in Afghanistan." The gemstone is lapis lazuli, dug in West Hindu Kush as early as 6,000 years ago and transported in Antiquity by old routes to remote regions of the three continents of the Old World. Lailuma Noori writes that the Route is still only a project to be implemented.

Kakar, Javed Hamim; President
Noori, Lailuma; New
Shadi, Khan Saif; Afghanistan
Salehi, Zarghona; Ghani
The Kabul Times; Azure

2.11 Golden Eagle Luxury Trains

A British travel agency with the headquarters in Altrincham, near Manchester. For 25 years now, the agency has organised long-distance luxury tourist trips across Europe, Asia, Africa and South America. One of them is a "Silk Road" expedition from Moscow to Beijing via Volgograd, the Karakum Desert, Khiva, Ashgabat, Merv, Bukhara, Samarkand, Tashkent, Alma Ata, Turfan, Dunghuang and Xian. The trip, naturally, involves stays and sightseeing at important locations of the old Silk road. On offer are also other trips, such as the Trans-Siberian Express from Moscow to Vladivostok, the Trans-Mongolian Express from Moscow to Ulan Bator and the Persian Odyssey from Moscow to Tehran.

Golden Eagle Luxury Trains

2.12 Grzelak, Tomasz

Chairman of the Board of Hatrans Logistics, a Lodz-based company which operates the freight train service from Lodz to Chengdu, initiated in 2013. Michał Frąk explains: "Tomasz Grzelak has managed to set up the first regular freight train line between Poland and China." Bogdan Możdżyński poetically calls the project "Tomasz Grzelak's Chinese dream." The first experimental shipment that crossed the frontier station of Małaszewice on New Year's Eve of 2012 is described by Grzelak himself in the following way: "We really wanted the train to enter Poland still in 2012. That is why we were deep up to here in paperwork on New Year's Eve. We needed over three thousand seals on our papers. I drove nearly a hundred kilometres simply by driving all over the terminal and handling the formalities."

Frąk, Michał; Polak
Możdżyński, Bogdan; Chiński

2.13 Guangdong Maritime Silk Road Museum
(海上丝绸之路博物馆)

A museum located on the Hailing Island in the Chinese city of Yangjiang on the coast of the South China Sea. Opened on 24 December, 2009, the museum can present about 300,000 exhibits made available to tourists and researchers across its nearly 20,000 m^2 space. The main exhibit of "the museum (...) dedicated to China's History of Ocean Civilization and Maritime Trade" is the Nanhai One, a wreck of a wooden merchant ship which sailed along the maritime Silk Road in the Song dynasty period (1127–1279). Discovered in the sea near the museum in 1987, the 24.5-metre-long and 9.8-metre-wide vessel is preserved in good shape. It is likely to have contained about 70,000 objects, chiefly china for export.

China Heritage Newsletter; China
Travel China Guide; Guangdong
UNESCO; Maritime
UNESCO; The UNESCO Silk

2.14 Hatrans Logistics Ltd.

A Lodz-based company providing national and international freight services: shipment, storage and customs formalities. Since 2013, it has operated a regular, weekly railway line between Chengdu, China, and Lodz, Poland (see 1.1.2.). According to the company's data, "each train consists of 41 cars loaded with 40 containers. The travel (...) takes 14 days." In 2015, the company started also a train service from Lodz to

China's Xiamen (see 1.1.3.). In November, 2014, at the Poland-China Economic Forum in Shanghai, Hatrans signed a contract with the Chinese company Unishunf Investments concerning the construction of a new logistics centre in Lodz.

Hatrans Logistics
Woźniak, Adam; Z Łódzkiego

2.15 International Dunhuang Project

A British Library project launched in 1994: "Its aim was to preserve and make accessible to everyone archaeological artefacts from the eastern part of the great trade routes of the pre-modern era, the Silk Road of the first millennium AD." Institutions based in 12 countries are involved in the project. Among them are:

Bibliothèque nationale de France, Paris,
Guimet Museum, Paris,
Research Institute of Korean Studies, Seoul,
Ryukoku University, Kyoto,
The Berlin-Brandenburg Academy of Science and Humanities, Berlin,
The British Library, London,
The British Museum, London,
The Dunhuang Academy, Dunhuang,
The Institute for Oriental Manuscripts, Petersburg,
The Library of the Hungarian Academy of Sciences, Budapest,
The Museum for Asian Art, Berlin,
The National Library of China, Beijing, and
The Victoria & Albert Museum, London.

Arts & Humanities Research Council; The Silk
The International Dunhuang Project; The Silk

2.16 International North-South Transport Corridor

An international agreement concluded by Iran, India and Russia in Petersburg, Russia, on 12 September, 2000, to develop a transportation route linking the Indian Ocean to North-European countries via Iran and Russia.

The project was joined by Armenia, Azerbaijan, Belarus, Bulgaria, Kazakhstan, Kyrgyzstan, Oman, Syria, Tajikistan, Turkey and Ukraine. Crucial to the Corridor was also the Ashgabat Agreement of April 2012, signed by Iran, Qatar, Oman, Turkmenistan and Uzbekistan, and later joined by Kazakhstan and India. Consisting of several segments, the Corridor involves various transportation modes: 1. a maritime connection between the ports of Mumbai, India, and Bandar Abbas, Iran; 2. land routes between Bandar Abbas and Iran's ports on the Caspian Sea; 3. sea shipping between Iran's ports and the Caspian Sea ports of Russia and Kazakhstan; 4. overland transportation via Kazakhstan and Russia to Petersburg on the Baltic Sea and North European countries. One of the Corridor's crucial investments is the Iran-Turkmenistan-Kazakhstan railway line opened on 3 December, 2014. The official opening was attended by President of Turkmenistan Gurbanguly Berdymukhammedov and President of Kazakhstan Nursultan Nazarbayev. Connecting the three countries by train was made possible by the construction of railway tracks from Gorgan (Persian: گرگان) in North Iran, via Bereket in Turkmenistan, to Janaozen (Ozen) (Kazakh: Жаңаөзен) in Kazakhstan.

International Law Office; Bi-Weekly Newsletter
Bipul, Chatterjee; Singh Surendar; An Opportunity
International North-South Transport
Railway Gazette; Iran
Talmiz, Ahmad; Who's
The Hans India; Ashgabat

2.17 Islamic Development Bank (البنك الإسلامي للتنمية)

An international financial institution with the headquarters in Jeddah, Saudi Arabia, assembling 57 countries, mainly from Asia and Africa, but also Europe's Albania and America's Suriname. The Bank's major shareholders are: Saudi Arabia, Libya, Iran, Nigeria, the United Arab Emirates, Qatar, Egypt, Kuwait and Turkey. The Bank was "established in accordance with Articles of Agreement done at the City of Jeddah, Kingdom of Saudi Arabia on 24/7/1394 (12/8/1974), signed and ratified by all member countries (…). The purpose of the Bank is to foster the economic development and social progress of member countries and Muslim communities individually as well as jointly in accordance with the principles of Sharia," i.e. Islamic Law. The Bank is implementing the Enhanced Competitiveness Increased Trade and Economic Growth programme for Central Asia for 2016–2020. It funds ventures such as the Silk Road Project Azerbaijan, aimed to modernise Azerbaijan's railways for the TRACECA Project of a transportation corridor between Europe and Asia via the Caucasus.

Islamic Development Bank
Islamic Development Bank; Silk
Islamic Development Bank Group; Special

2.18 Li, Keqiang (李克强)

Vice Premier of the People's Republic of China in 2008–13 and Premier since 15 March, 2015. He has visited many countries popularising and implementing the policy of "a new corridor of mutual connections." He took part, among others, in the Third Meeting of Heads of Government of China and Central and Eastern European Countries in Belgrade on 16–17 November, 2014, where he explained: "To build a China-Europe land-sea express line has become a highlight for major-project co-operation between China and the 16 CEECs. A convenient and efficient connectivity network that spans across Asia and Europe has always been the dream of countries in this region. The 'Belt and Road Initiative' China has proposed aims at working with other countries to make this dream come true." Besides Serbia, he has also travelled to Angola, Belgium, Brazil, Brunei, Chile, Colombia, Ethiopia, France, Germany, Great Britain, Hungary, India, Ireland, Italy, Kenya, Malaysia, Nigeria, Pakistan, Peru, Romania, Russia, Switzerland, Thailand, Uzbekistan and Vietnam.

Belgrade Meeting, Belgrade
MacDowall, Andrew; China
Szczudlik-Tatar, Justyna; China's

2.19 Maersk (A.P. Møller-Mærsk A/S)

One of the largest global sea cargo transportation companies with the headquarters in Copenhagen, Denmark. A leader in container shipping. It owns, for example, several huge, 400-metre-long Maersk Triple E container ships with a capacity of 18,000 TEU each. The company has signed an agreement with China's Qingdao Port Group to build a new port terminal in Vado Ligure in the Bay of Genoa, Italy. The terminal is due to be operational in 2018. Tim Smith of the Maersk Group North Asia called the enterprise an example of partnership within the Belt and Road initiative.

Maersk
Salvacion, Manny; Maersk

2.20 Mausam Project

A project presented by India's Minister of Culture Shri Ravindra Singh at the 38th session of the World Heritage Committee in Doha, Qatar, on 20 June, 2014, in an attempt to have the maritime routes of the Indian Ocean inscribed in UNESCO's World Heritage List. The ambassadors of China, Iran, Qatar, Myanmar, Vietnam and the United Arab Emirates expressed an interest in the initiative. Heading the project, Joy Kuriakose explains that "at the macro level it aims to re-connect and re-establish communications between countries of the Indian Ocean world, which would lead to an enhanced understanding of cultural values and concerns; while at the micro level the focus is on understanding national cultures in their regional maritime milieu." "Mausam" (Hindu मौसम) means "monsoon" – a seasonal wind enabling navigation. The project strives to re-construct the network of maritime connections which, since antiquity, has integrated East Africa, the Arab Peninsula, Iran and the countries of South and South-Eastern Asia. As India once played the key role in the network, some people believe that the initiative embodies a striving to reinstate the Republic of India as a crucial power in the Indian Ocean region. Yet, *The Hans India* insists that "Project 'Mausam' is not aimed to counter China's Silk Route strategy." With the Ministry of Culture, the National Museum and the Gandhi National Centre for the Arts as India's major actors in the project, it involves lectures, conferences, exhibitions and publications.

Kuriakose, Joy; Project
Pillalamarri, Akhilesh; Project
Simply Decoded; Project
The Hans India; What

2.21 National Development and Reforms Commission (NDRC) (中华人民共和国国家发展和改革委员会)

A Beijing-based institution accountable to the PRC State Council. Since March 2013, the Commission has been headed by Shaoshi Xu. One of its major goals is developing the country's macroeconomic policy. On 30 March, 2015, the NDRC published a document titled *Vision and Actions on Jointly Building "Silk Road Economic Belt and 21st-Century Maritime Silk Road"*,[5] which details China's new initiative. Its introduction states: "For thousands of years, the Silk Road Spirit – 'peace and cooperation, openness and inclusiveness, mutual learning and mutual benefit' – has been passed from generation to generation, promoted the progress of human civilization, and contributed greatly to the prosperity and development of the countries along the Silk Road. Symbolising communication and cooperation between the East and the West, the Silk Road Spirit is a historic and cultural heritage shared by all countries around the world."

National Development and Reform Commission[6]
NDRC; Vision

2.22 New Development Bank (NDB)

An international bank established in Frotaleza, Brazil, on 15 July, 2014, by an agreement signed by the BRICS countries, i.e. Brazil, Russia, India, China and the Republic of South Africa. The Bank's headquarters are located in Shanghai, its official language is English and its current President is Kundapur Vaman Kamath of India (as of 2017). The Bank itself defines its aim as "mobiliz[ing] resources for infrastructure and sustainable development projects in BRICS and other emerging economies, as well as in developing countries." The Bank's Vice President Leslie Maasdorp cites figures showing that its founding countries make up "43% of the world's population and generate roughly 22% of global GDP."

Maasdorp, Leslie; What
New Development Bank; Changing

---

5   Henceforth the documnet will be referred to as the *Vision*.
6   Henceforth, the Commission will be acronymically referred to as NDRC in entry references.

2.23 New Silk Road Company Ltd. (NSRC)

The Company operates the Dubai International Finance Center (DIFC), which "is a global financial centre strategically located between the East and West." Its aim is to "contribute to Dubai's reputation as a global business hub by maintaining international standards [and] developing international relations." A special free economic zone of over 110 acres was established in Dubai in 2004, based on the federal law of the United Arab Emirates, which gave it an autonomous legal system. Besides financial institutions, the Centre area houses also luxury shops, restaurants, cafes, art galleries and hotels. Both the NSRC and the DIFC are headed by Essa Kazim, who is also Chairman of Borse Dubai.

Four Seasons Hotel Dubai
New Silk Road Company Ltd.

2.24 New Silk Road Group Ltd.

A Chinese company based in Dongguan in the Pearl River's mouth to the South Chinese Sea. Founded in 2006, it is a manufacturer of silk, silk-cotton, silk-linen and silk-viscose fabrics. Its four plants employ 600 workers. The company exports its produce to countries in six continents.

New Silk Road Group

2.25 New Silk Road Institute Prague

Set up in September 2015, the institution defines its aim as contributing "to the promotion of ideas that increase mutually beneficial cooperation between Asian and European countries, as well as searching for new ways of communication and economic cooperation within the concept of New Silk Road. Above all, the Institute aims to assist in building the world of communication, not the world of purposeless confrontation."

New Silk Road Institute Prague

2.26 New Silk Road Investment

A Singapore-based financial investment company founded in 2008 and headed by Raymond Goh. The company states: "We invest in Asian companies with the aim of achieving superior long term absolute returns through

an independent, fundamentally-based, value-driven investment process."
The company is the manager of the Asia Landmark Fund Ltd., offered to
international investor through its agency in the Cayman Islands.

Asia Landmark Fund LTD
New Silk Road Investment

2.27 Ni, Peimin (倪培民)

Professor of Philosophy at the Grand Valley State University in Allendale,
Michigan, US. Among his publications is "The Underlying Philosophy and
Impact of the New Silk Road World Order," in which he explains the philosophical underpinnings of China's New Silk Road policy. He clarifies also
that the project involves also constructing the "Silk Road World Order"
(in brief the "Silk World Order"), that is a new "silk" order of the world
drawing on Confucius's Chinese philosophy and the even older tradition of
tianxia (天下), i.e. common destiny shared by everything beneath the sky.

Grand Valley State University; Peimin
Ni, Peimin; The Underlying
Shanghai Academy of Social Sciences; Professor

2.28 Park, Kyong

Architect, artist, theorist and professor at the Visual Arts Department, University of California in San Diego. One of his exhibitions was *The New Silk
Road* at the Museo de Arte Contemporaneo de Castilla y León in León,
Spain. Since 2007, he has run the New Silk Roads research project exploring
the changes in Asia's towns and regions between Istanbul and Tokyo and
focused on such issues as migration, the rise of supra-national institutions,
social and spatial outcomes of globalisation and electronic information
exchange. So far, three field trips have been organised within the project.
Held from July to October 2007, the first of them involved Shanghai, Singapore, Seoul, Tokyo, Guangzhou, Foshan, Dongguan, Shenzhen, Hong
Kong, Macau and Beijing; the second, held from December 2007 to January
2008, went from Istanbul via Delhi to Dubai; and the third, in September
2008, focused on Bukhara, Samarkand, Tashkent, Alma Ata and Astana.

New Silk Roads
Redcat; Kyong

2.29 Putin, Vladimir Vladimirovich (Владимир Владимирович Путин)

President of the Russian Federation in 1999–2008 and since 7 May, 2012, till the present moment (as of 2017). He is involved in building the Eurasian Economic Union (EAEU) (Евразийский экономический союз). Signing a treaty establishing the Union, together with President of Kazakhstan Nursultan Nazarbayev and President of Belarus Aleksandr Lukashenko, he said: "Our geographic location makes it possible to create transportation and logistics routes of not only regional, but also global significance and attract large-scale trade from Europe and Asia." In 2015, the Union was joined by Armenia and Kyrgyzstan. During a meeting with Jinping Xi at Moscow's Kremlin on 8 May, 2015, Vladimir Putin stated: "We think that the Eurasian integration project and the Silk Road Economic Belt project complement each other very harmoniously." In his speech to the UN General Assembly in New York on 26 September, 2015, he presented an idea of "integration of integrations," which envisions not only cooperation between the EAEU and China's new initiative but also collaboration between the EAEU and the European Union. On the occasion, he spoke about Russia's plans "to interconnect the Eurasian economic union, and China's initiative of the Silk Road economic belt."

President of Russia; Press
President of Russia; Treaty
Putin, Wladymir; U.N.
Putin, Wladymir; Press
Starr, S. Frederick; Svante E. Cornell (red.); Putin's
The Voice of Russia; Russian
Zhao, Minghao; China's

2.30 Richthofen, Ferdinand von

Professor of Geology at the Friedrich Wilhelm University of Berlin (1833–1905). In 1860–1872, he travelled and did research in Eastern Asia, including China. He is considered to have coined the term "Silk Road" to describe contacts between China and the West. In his article in The Silk Road, Daniel Waugh explains that the very title of Richthofen's study *Über die zentralasiatischen Seidenstraßen bis zum 2. Jh. n. Chr* [On Central Asia's Silk-Roads up to the 2nd century AD] (Berlin, 1877) contains the German word "Seidenstraße" derived from *serica* – the ancient Roman (Latin) term denoting silk's country of origin, i.e. China.

Waugh, Daniel; Richthofen's

2.31 Shanghai Cooperation Organisation (SCO)

Set up on in Shanghai, on 15 June, 2001, the Organisation assembles China, India, Kazakhstan, Kyrgyzstan, Pakistan, Russia, Tajikistan and Uzbekistan. The observer status has been granted to Afghanistan, Belarus, Iran and Mongolia. The SCO's headquarters are located in Beijing. Eleanor Albert writes that while initially the Organisation was chiefly dedicated to building mutual trust and demilitarising the borders, it has now "intensified its focus on regional economic initiatives, like the recently announced integration of the China-led Silk Road Economic Belt and the Russia-led Eurasian Economic Union."

Albert, Eleanor; The Shanghai
Shanghai Cooperation Organization

2.32 Shevardnadze, Eduard (Georgian: ედუარდ შევარდნაძე, Russian: Эдуáрд Шеварднáдзе)

A Georgian politician, Minister of Foreign Affairs of the USSR under Mikhail Gorbachev and President of Georgia in 1995–2003. He died in 2014. In the aftermath of the USSR collapse, he developed a "Great Silk Road" concept as a new vision of the development of post-USRR countries, with Georgia playing the first fiddle. Initially, the project foucsed on the construction of pipelines to transport natural gas and crude oil from the Caspian Sea region to Turkey and Europe. Later, Shevardnadze developed his concept to give it a more comprehensive economic and political resonance. During a meeting with DaimlerChrysler's CEO Chrysler Klaus Meier on 16 September, 2003, he spoke about reviving the "Great Silk Road" and declared "Our dream has come true," pointing to the regional cooperation and interest from the US, Japan and European countries. Irena Cheng writes that Eduard Shevardnadze thought of the Great Silk Road not only in the economic terms but also as a "route of tolerance."

Azerbaijan State News Agency; Eduard
Cheng, Irene; The New

Gegeshidze, Archil; The New
Partridge, Ben; Georgia

2.33 Silk Road Cultural Journey

On 19 September 2014, a special ceremony was organised in Jingyang, central China's Shaanxi Province, by the local government and local tea companies. A caravan of 136 two-humped Bactrian camels and over 100 human travellers wearing ancient costumes set off with a cargo of tea along the Silk Road, scheduled to reach Kazakhstan one year later. As no information about the completion of the travel could be found, it stands to reason to suppose that the caravan was lost underway, along with its load of tea, likely not the first incident of this kind the Silk Road has seen.

China Daily; Silk

2.34 Silk Road Film Festival

Organised by Carla Mooney, Steinar Oli and Jonsson and Delwyn Mooney, the festival has been held in Dublin, Ireland, in March since 2014. The organisers call themselves a small group of volunteers and aficionados and describe the festival as "celebrat[ing] cinema, culture and art, presenting films from countries which were once part of the historical network of the Silk Road ancient trade routes." Film screenings are accompanied by discussions and seminars. The festival is funded by private sponsors and the Irish government.

Silk Road Film Festival

2.35 Silk Road Foundation (USA)

A non-profit organisation with the seat in Saratoga, California, US. The Foundation frames itself as "the bridge for cultural exchange and appreciation between Eastern and Western cultures." Founded in 1996 "to promote the study and preservation of cultures and art on Inner Asia and the Silk Road," the Foundation "operates from private funding and donations." Among other activities, it runs an Internet information platform about Silk Road research and publishes *The Silk Road* journal.

Silk Road Foundation (USA)
The Silk Road, vol. 13, 2015

2.36 Silk Road Foundation (Korea)

Founded in Seoul, South Korea, in 2005, the organisation says it "is a non-profit organization that was launched to practice mutual sharing and cultural communication for a New Silk Road in the 21st century among Eurasian, Central Asian and East Asian countries. The foundation is committed to supporting social, economic and cultural communication among the scattered countries in the Silk Road region in order to maintain a cooperative relationship." The Foundation's Chairman Kim Won-ho said: "The old Silk Road connected the East to facilitate commerce and exchanges of cultures and new ideas. We want to help create a new Silk Road, which will connect people from different countries." The Foundation co-finances meetings, conferences and projects. Attending the Foundation's assembly in Seoul on 23 September, 2008, the Ambassador of Turkey to South Korea, Deniz Ozmen, stated that the New Silk Road could contribute to the economic development and that Turkey formed its other terminus.

Kim, Se-jeong; S. Korea
Silk Road Foundation (Korea)

2.37 Silk Road Fund

Registered in Beijing on 29 December, 2014, and chaired by Jin Qi, the institution was set up to manage the fund of $40 billion, which the PRC plans to use to finance the projects of the Silk Road Economic Belt and the 21st-Century Maritime Silk Road. Jinping Xi said about the Fund that, besides investing its own capital, it was going to encourage investors from Asia and other parts of the world to get actively involved in its projects. One of them is, for example, the construction of the China-Pakistan Economic Corridor to connect Pakistan's port of Gwadar to the Sinciang-Uyghur Autonomous Region, China.

Consortium Chemico
Silk Road Found
Xinhuanet; Silk

2.38 Silk Road Gold Fund

A fund established in May 2015 by the Shanghai Gold Exchange. Its main shareholders are China's two largest gold-mining companies the Shandong Gold Group (35% of shares) and the Shaanxi Gold Group (25%). Xisheng

Tang of The Industrial Fund Management said that "the Fund will invest in gold mining in countries along the Silk Road." According to the Xinhua agency, the Fund is to help the central banks of the New Silk Road countries purchase gold in order to increase their gold reserves. The Shanghai Gold Exchange was set up in 2002 by the People's Bank of China to control precious metals trading. Ekaterina Blinova believes that both the Shanghai Gold Exchange as well as its funds and other solutions serve to build a new, post-dollar monetary world order and to peg the Chinese yuan to gold.

Blinova, Ekaterina; Gold
Engdahl, F. William; China
Xinhua, China

2.39 Silk Road Group (SRG)

A private investment company set up in 1990 with the seat in Tbilisi, Georgia. The company declares: "Since its inception, the Silk Road Group has enjoyed the steady growth by revitalizing traditional trade routes, which had been neglected for decades. (…) The company started its business activities with transportation and trading of commodities in the Central Asian and Caucasus regions and has established itself as a leader in the rail transportation of the liquid and dry cargoes." In 2000, the company established the Commercial Bank Silk Road, which was transformed into the Silk Road Bank in 2015. The Group's other enterprise is Silknet, an Internet, phone and television operator.

Silk Road Group
Silk Road Group; Transportation

2.40 Silk Road International Arts Festival

A culture festival in Xi'an held by the Culture Department of the Shaanxi Province. Hosting a number of events, the Festival's first edition took place on 7 September, 2015, and its second edition on 12 September, 2016. The CC. TV channel informs: "The Tang-Dynasty capital of China, Chang'an – known today as Xi'an – was gloriously enriched by the ancient Silk Road, making it a fitting location for the Second Silk Road International Arts Festival."

CC.TV; Silk
China Daily; Opening
The Silk Road International

2.41 Silk Road Railway

A 30-days' railway trip organised by Sundowners Overland, a travel agency in Melbourne, Australia: "From Istanbul – gateway to the East, first to Iran, which will surprise and reward every visitor with its warm welcome and the incredible monuments and architecture of Isfahan, and then across the Karakum Desert and Turkmenistan to the fabled Silk Road cities of Samarkand and Bukhara. Finally, across the Tian Shan mountains to the oases of China's Taklamakan Desert – and the eastern terminus of the great silk road – Xian, ancient Chang'an, the glittering capital of ancient Cathay, and on to Beijing, the modern-day capital of China."

Silk Road Railway
Sundowners Overland; Sharing

2.42 Silk Road Reporters

A Washington-based independent news agency set up on 1 January, 2014. The agency publishes online political, economic and social news concerning Central Asia. It defines its mission as providing reports and analyses on Central Asia and relies on independent correspondents from Central Asia and the Caucasus region.

Silk Road Reporters

2.43 Silk Road Treasure Tours

A travel agency with the seat in Chester, New Jersey, US, founded and managed by Zulya Rajabova. The agency specialises in trips along the Silk Road to Central Asia, the Caucasus region, Mongolia and China. One of them is advertised as an "Authentic Silk Road Journey of a Lifetime," takes 34 days to complete and costs from $17,600 per person. The itinerary includes locations such as Turkey's Istanbul, Turkmenistan's Ashgabat, Mary and Merv, Uzbekistan's Bukhara, Samarkand, Khiva and Tashkent, Kyrgyzstan's Bishkek, village of Kochkor, Song Kul Lake, caravanserai Tash Rabat, Torugart Pass and China's Kashgar, Hoten, Urumqi, Turfan, Dunhuang, Lanzhou, Xian and Beijing.

Silk Road Treasure Tours

2.44 Silk Route Rail

A Hong Kong-based company headed by Darryl Hadaway, offering freight rail connections from three Chinese cities: Chongqing, Chengdu and Wuhan, to sixteen cities in Asia and Europe: Moscow/Alma Ata (4–9 days), Warsaw, Prague and Budapest (10–14 days), Hamburg/Duisburg/Vienna (11–15 days), Antwerp/Rotterdam/Copenhagen (12–16 days), Paris/London (13–17 days) and Basel/Milan/Rome/Istanbul (14–18 days). The company states that its aim is to connect communities living in the Silk Road Economic Belt.

Silk Route Rail
The Emergence of The Silk

2.45 Transport Corridor Europe-Caucasus-Asia (TRACECA)

An international collaboration programme established by the Ministers of Transport and Trade of Armenia, Azerbaijan, Georgia, Kazakhstan, Kyrgyzstan, Turkmenistan and Uzbekistan, with the support of the European Union, in Brussels in May 1993. Its aim is to develop a transport corridor connecting Europe and Central Asia via the Black Sea, the Caucasus and the Caspian Sea. Since its inception, the programme has been joined by Ukraine, Mongolia, Moldova (1996–1998), Bulgaria, Romania, Turkey (2000), Iran and Lithuania (2009). One of the programme's multiple conferences held on 8 September, 1998, in Baku and titled *TRACECA – Restoration of the Historic Silk Route* was attended by the Presidents of Azerbaijan, Bulgaria, Georgia, Kyrgyzstan, Moldova, Romania, Turkey, Ukraine and Uzbekistan, experts from thirty-two countries and representatives of twelve international organisations. The meeting resulted in the Basic Multilateral Agreement on International Transport for Development of the Corridor Europe-Caucasus-Asia. The Agreement concerns collaboration on the construction and development of railroads, highways, telecommunications and pipelines. The programme's Permanent Secretariat is based in Baku. On its current website (as of 2017), the organisation calls itself TRACECA – The Silk Road of the 21st century.

Partridge, Ben; Georgia
TRACECA

2.46 UNCTAD

The United Nations Conference on Trade and Development with the seat in Geneva, founded by the UN member states in 1964. Among its many activities supporting the economic development of developing countries and their integration with the world's economy, the conference boasts its own New Silk Road programme. For example, it has published the *Investment Guide to the Silk Road*, which deals with five Central Asian countries (Kazakhstan, Kyrgyzstan, Tajikistan, Turkmenistan and Uzbekistan) and four western provinces of China (Gansu, Ningxia, Shaanxi and Sinciang), discussing their development opportunities in tourism, power industry, mining, transport, agriculture, machine industry and IT.

UNCTAD;
UNCTAD; Investment

2.47 UNESCO Silk Road

A programme started by the United Nations Educational, Scientific and Cultural Organisation in 1988 "to contribute to the promotion of mutual understanding, intercultural dialogue, reconciliation and cooperation among nations and people sharing the Silk Roads common heritage." The programme includes field research, resource archiving, symposia, exhibitions and publications. Fifty-five countries participate in the project, with special support from Kazakhstan and Germany. Part of the programme is also an Internet information portal called the UNESCO Silk Road Online Platform. It announces: "The historic Silk Roads were a network of trade routes (...) along which people of many different cultures, religions and languages met, exchanged ideas and influenced each other. It is this unique history of mutual exchange and dialogue that the Silk Road Online Platform seeks to promote, in line with the 2013–2022 International Decade for the Rapprochement of Cultures and as part of UNESCO's commitment to creating a culture of peace."

UNESCO; Reviving
UNESCO; The UNESCO Silk

2.48 Xi, Jinping (习近平)

Since 15 November, 2012, Secretary General of the Communist Party of China and since 14 March, 2013, President of the People's Republic of

China. Nadège Rolland observes that his policies mainly aim to "to restore China's pre-nineteenth century grandeur and influence in order to make it a 'prosperous, strong, culturally advanced and harmonious country.'" During his visit to Astana, Kazakhstan, on 7 September, 2013, Jinping Xi presented his Silk Road Economic Belt project, and travelling to Indonesia in October, 2013, he put forward another project – The 21st-Century Maritime Silk Road. The former focuses on overland communications and cooperation while the latter on maritime communications and collaboration. Ever since their inception, the two projects have been viewed as mutually complementary and referred to jointly as "One Belt, One Road" (OBOR, 一带一路) or the "Belt and Road." Marcin Kaczmarski insists that "the concept of the road is a personal project of China's new leader Jinping Xi." Speaking at the Nursultan Nazarbayev University in Astana, Kazakhstan, on 7 September 2013, Jinping Xi said: "To forge closer economic ties, deepen cooperation and expand development in the Euro-Asia region, we should take an innovative approach and jointly build an 'economic belt' along the silk road. This will be a great undertaking benefitting the people of all countries along the route." And in a speech, he gave in Indonesia's Parliament in Jakarta on 2 October, 2013, he listed the following goals of the China-backed new policy:

1. build trust and develop good-neighbourliness;
2. work for win-win cooperation;
3. stand together and assist each other;
4. enhance mutual understanding and friendship;
5. stick to openness and inclusiveness.

Kaczmarski, Marcin; Nowy
Ministry of Foreign Affairs of the People's Republic of China; President
Rolland, Nadège; China's
Xi, Jinping; Silk
Xi, Jinping; Speech by Chinese President
Zhao, Minghao; China's

2.49 Yazıcı, Hayati

Turkish Minister of Trade and Customs. Vladimir Fedorenko regards him as the founder of the Turkish Silk Road project, presented at the International Forum on the Role of Customs Administration in Promoting and

Facilitating Trade among Silk Road Countries, held in Antalya, Turkey, in 2008. The Forum was attended by participants from seventeen countries (e.g. Azerbaijan, China, Georgia, India, Iran, Iraq, Kazakhstan, Kyrgyzstan, Mongolia, Russia, Syria, Tajikistan, Turkey and Uzbekistan), who discussed simplifying border-crossing procedures to smoothen international trade. The final outcome of the Forum was the Antalya Declaration, which has come to serve as the basis of further international collaboration. The Turkish project, labelled as the Silk Road Customs Cooperation Initiative, paved the way for the Caravanserai Project adopted at the following Forum in Baku in 2009, which concerned the construction of border-crossing points.

Fedorenko, Vladymir; The New
Yazıcı, Hayati; Turkey

2.50 Zepp-LaRouche, Helga

A German political activist, founder and head of the Schiller Institute (Washington, US). Since the early 1990s, she has developed the World Land-Bridge concept, which she has discussed on several occasions, therein in Beijing on 7–9 May, 1996, at the Renmin University on 29 September, 2015, and in numerous publications. The concept focuses on developing the communication infrastructure and, consequently, economic, political and cultural links among societies for the good and prosperity of humankind. Helga Zepp-LaRouche considers the new Chinese project to be an implementation of her concept; hence the title of her co-edited volume *The New Silk Road Becomes the World Land-Bridge*. She can be regarded as a pioneer of conceptualising the construction of communication infrastructure as a form of promoting international cooperation for peace and prosperity. She believes that China's new project offers "a new model of cooperation among the nations of the world."

Douglas, Rachel; Michael Billington; Helga Zepp-LaRouche; The New
Jones, William; Zepp-LaRouche
The International Schiller Institute; Build
The World Land Bridge
Zepp-LaRouche, Helga; The New Silk Road Will

3. Meanings and values

3.1 Advantages

The advantages of involvement in the New Silk Road are evoked once and again. Iris C. Gonzales addresses advantages of the new Chinese project to the Philippines. Speaking at the International New Silk Road Forum and the 4th Poland-China Regional Forum in Warsaw, Poland's Prime Minister Beata Szydło said: "The New Silk Road means immense economic opportunities and advantages. It is our common way to development." Paul Vandenberg and Khan Kikkawa attempt to explain the magical appeal of advantages promised to the New Road participants by referring to the global value chain that connects people, institutions and companies across the world and helps achieve outcomes unattainable without such remote relationships. The *Vision* cites benefits no fewer that thirteen times, including mutual advantages, profits to all the parties involved and even the fact that the new project "will benefit people around the world." Helga Zepp-LaRouche also believes that the New Silk Road "conforms to the common interests of human civilization." Nake Kamrany concurs, writing about "Sharing Global Prosperity Through Connectivity of the Silk Route Countries."

Gonzales, Iris C.; Philippines
Kamrany, Nake; China's
NDRC; Vision
Vandenberg, Paul; Khan Kikkawa; Global
WPolityce.Pl; Premier
Zepp-LaRouche, Helga; The New Silk Road Will

3.2 Afro-Eurasia[7]

The *Vision* published by the National Development and Reforms Commission of the PRC addresses "routes of trade and cultural exchanges that linked the major civilizations of Asia, Europe and Africa, collectively called

---

7   Some meanings, senses and values are evoked frequently while other ones less so when the New Silk Road is addressed. For this reason, the entries differ in length, with more attention devoted to those which recur in speeches, documents, advertisements and commentaries.

the Silk Road by later generations." Like many other authors, Theresa Fallon illustrates her text on the New Silk Road with a map of three continents provided by the Chinese news agency Xinhua. Justin Yifu Lin calls the concept outlined in the Chinese document "One Belt, One Road, One Continent." The term Afro-Eurasia as designating the geographical space of the New Silk Road has been used in many studies, for example by Paul Kielstra. It is also applied by the researchers of the old Silk Road to emphasise the unity of the communication network integrating distant regions of the Old World's three continents.

Andrea, Alfred J.; Scott C. Levi; The Silk
Fallon, Theresa; The New
Kielstra, Paul; The New
Lin, Justin Yifu; Industry
NDRC; Vision

3.3 Asia

The Asian Development Bank, which funds several projects under the umbrella term of the New Silk Road, defines itself as "Asian in character." In turn, the financial company New Silk Road Investment regards Asia and Asianness as economic assets in its investment strategy: "We invest in Asian companies with the aim of achieving superior long term absolute returns."

Asian Development Bank
Asia Landmark Fund LTD
New Silk Road Investment

3.4 Balance

The *Vision* states that the initiative aims to secure the "balanced and sustainable development" of all its participating countries. Minghao Zhao writes that a proportionate economic development of China's western and eastern provinces is also one of the project's objectives. The latter, which now seriously lag behind, are to benefit from new connections built with Central Asian countries under the project. Alice Ekman considers the overall goal to be "the creation of a 'balanced regional economic cooperation architecture,'" where economy is not the only focal point. David Cohen cites China's Minister of Foreign Affairs Yi Wang, who believes that "Western economies, and mainly the US, were responsible for the global economic and political imbalances that led to the global financial crisis. China should work to 'rebalance' (再平衡, *zai pingheng*) these imbalances through the OBOR." What is at stake is not just the balanced development of Chinese provinces, other countries or Central Asia, but also of the entire world as such.

Cohen, David; China
Ekman, Alice; China
NDRC; Vision
Zhao, Minghao; China's

3.5 Bridge

There are many bridges along the Silk Road. There is a bridge across the border river Panj, funded by the US, and another one, built by the China Road and Bridge Corporation on the Danube in Serbia. In California, US, the Silk Road Foundation wants to be the "bridge between Eastern and Western cultures," and Turkey's "Anatolia has been a bridge between the East and the West." One hears in Warsaw that "Poland is to serve as a bridge to Europe for China," and Nepal is envisioned as a "'land bridge' between India and China" by Pradumna Rana and Wai-Mun Chia. Chinese Premier Jiabao Wen, in turn, insists that "cultural exchanges are a bridge connecting the hearts and minds of people of all countries" while to Helga Zepp-LaRouche the entire "New Silk Road Becomes the World Land-Bridge."

BBC News; US-made
Radio Warszawa; Polska
Rana, Pradumna B.; Wai-Mun Chia; The Revival
Serbia Construction; Chinese
Silk Road Foundation
UNESCO Silk Road; Turkey
Wen, Jiabao; Our
Zepp-LaRouche, Helga; Michael Billington; Rachel Douglas; The New

3.6 China

Discussing the New Silk Road, Justyna Szczudlik-Tatar highlights the "Chinese Dream." Thereby, she refers to Jinping Xi's words: "The great revival of the Chinese nation is the greatest Chinese dream." Speaking at the first session of the 12th National People's Congress in Beijing on 17 March, 2013, the President added also that in pursuing this dream China must act in its distinct Chinese way. The Chinese initiative of restoring the Silk Road seems both to be instrumental in making the Chinese Dream come true and to meet the criterion of being a typically Chinese way of pursuing the Dream. The news agency Xinhuanet explains that the Dream involves building a strong and advancing country, a revival of the nation and prosperity of the people. Strong and wealthy China is a value promoted by the New Silk Road. Another value lies in the specific "Chineseness" to be accomplished by the specifically Chinese character of the New Silk Road initiative, which is discussed by Jurij Kulincew (Юрий Кулинцев).

Szczudlik-Tatar, Justyna; China's
Xi, Jinping; Speech at the closing
Xinhuanet; Xi Jinping
Кулинцев, Юрий; Один

3.7 Communication

The term communication sometimes refers to roads, railway lines and maritime or flight connections. In other contexts, it designates entire corridors which include not only systems of the former, but also ports, free trade zones, pipelines, etc., such as the China-Pakistan Economic Corridor or the Transport Corridor Europe-Caucasus-Asia. The *Vision* highlights communication, cooperation and integration of and consultation among the countries involved in the new Chinese project, insisting that communication mechanisms foster mutual trust. In this context, communication means political dialogue among countries, envisaged not only as international agreements, but also as "communication between political parties and parliaments," which promotes "friendly exchanges between legislative bodies, major political parties and political organizations of countries along the Belt and Road." In India's Mausam Project, which aims to "re-establish communications between countries of the Indian Ocean world, which would lead to an enhanced understanding of cultural values and concerns," communication transcends the economy and politics to designate encounters of various cultures and their varied effects.

Georgian Ambassador Archil Gegeshidze regards the Great Silk Road as communication in the sense of relationships between East and West. Turkish Minister of Transport Binali Yildrim adds: "The Silk Road in not a caravan but rather a route linking western and eastern civilizations to one another." Yet, many of those who evoke the New Silk Road still believe that such communication is best emblematised by a traditional caravan of Bactrian camels, such as the one that traversed the streets of Jingyang in central China's Shaanxi Province during the Silk Road Cultural Journey festival on 19 September, 2014.

Asian Development Bank; The New
China Daily; Silk
Gegeshidze, Archil; The New
Kuriakose, Joy; Project
NDRC; Vision
HKTDT Research; The Belt, s. 2
Pillalamarri, Akhilesh; Project
Turksoy; The Conference

3.8 Community

Hilary Clinton evoked the community of the old Road and called for building a community of the New one: "Historically, the nations of South and Central Asia were connected to each other and the rest of the continent by a sprawling trading network called the Silk Road (...). Let's work together to create a new Silk Road." Addressing the New Road, Jinping Xi speaks of a community of interests: "We should take an innovative approach and jointly build an 'economic belt along the Silk Road'. This will be a great undertaking benefitting the people of all countries along the route." Yiwei Wang adds that the OBOR aims to build a "community of interests and security (利益+安全共同体, *liyi+anquan gorgonian*)." Theresa Fallon observes that the initiative envisages a "common destiny." Jurij Kulincew (Юрий Кулинцев) highlights the notion of "the community of destiny" that informs the Chinese project. Peimin Ni explains this in the following way: "Confucians are well known for their sense of seeing *tianxia* 天下, 'all under heaven,' as a community of shared destiny. As contemporary Chinese political philosopher Zhao Tingyang points out, the term *tianxia* represents an underlying philosophy totally different from the philosophy behind the notion of nation-state. *Tianxia* entails a sense of seeing all under the heaven as interconnected." Other commentators observe that, despite its financial, economic and political resources, China will not be able to implement the transcontinental, or even global, New Road without other countries' involvement. Citing Export-Import Bank of China analyst Changhui Zhao, Adam Kaliński says that "even though China is the leading party in the project, it will have to negotiate with other countries if the enterprise is to succeed."

Clinton, Hillary Rodham; Remarks
Fallon, Theresa; The New
Kaliński, Adam; Na nowy
Ni, Peimin; The Underlying
Wang, Yiwei; How; qtd. in: Bondaz, Antoine; Rebalancing
Xi, Jinping; Promote
Xi, Jinping; Speech by Chinese
Кулинцев, Юрий; Один

3.9 Cooperation

Cooperation appears in the titles of New Road conferences in Istanbul (2013) and Urumqi (2015). Jinping Xi highlighted the need of cooperation for the common good in Astana and Jakarta in 2013. The *Vision* mentions cooperation on over one hundred occasions in a variety of contexts; and the New Road project itself tends to be labelled "The Belt and Road cooperation." In Xi'an, The Silk Road International Arts Festival is held to disseminate cooperation worldwide as a precious idea of Chinese culture. Alice Ekman notices "new models of international cooperation," and Helga Zepp-LaRouche "a new model of cooperation among the nations of the world." Cooperation with China under the New Road scheme has been addressed on many occasions, for example, at the 4th Poland-China Economic Forum held in Katowice on 20–22 April, 2015. Citing Lijuan Liu, Jerzy Dudała states that "China wants the China-Poland cooperation to serve as a model of cooperation with Central and East-European countries." In 2011, the Asian Development Bank called its New Silk Road programme "cooperation for prosperity," as did Jinping Xi his project. Peimin Ni foregrounds two terms often used by the President. Side by side with a "community of shared destiny," he often evokes *hezuogongyin* 合作共赢 – "cooperation and co-prosperity": "If we are a community of shared destiny, then we have no option but to cooperate with each other."

3.10 Culture

Bonnie Glaser and Melissa Murphy report a debate of Chinese intellectuals and politicians which surrounded the germination of China's Road project. In 1993, Huning Wang, Director of the Policy Research Office of the CPC Central Committee, wrote: "If a country has an admirable culture and ideological system, other countries will tend to follow it." Glaser and Murphy explain that, at the CPC Congress in 1998, "president Jiang Zemin announced the decision on building socialist 'spiritual civilization'"; subsequently, an "'Outline on National Morality,' combining Chinese traditional values and socialist core values, was issued in 2001." In this way, China wanted to accomplish "the reevaluation of Chinese traditional culture" and "the rehabilitation of once vilified traditional schools of thought – Confucianism, Taoism, and Buddhism" for the "socialist core value system." One year later, Yunshan Liu wrote about the "power of culture" and "socialist culture with Chinese characteristics" as "a powerful attraction and inspiration not only to the Chinese people, but to the people throughout the world." The following President of the PRC Jintao Hu stated in 2007 that China should "enhance culture as part of the soft power of our country," and Premier Jiabao Wen declared: "We should expand cultural exchanges with other countries. Cultural exchanges are a bridge connecting the hearts and minds of people of all countries." In the same year, however, Jian Hu of the Shanghai Academy of Social Sciences pointed to the "the deficit in China's 'cultural trade' with the West." Glaser and Murphy describe

Chinese intellectuals as believing that "soft power can secure a stable and peaceful international environment and facilitate the acceptance of China's rise internationally." Peimin Ni, who analyses the philosophical underpinnings of the Chinese Road project, observes that its "philosophical insight is deeply rooted in the traditional Chinese culture," including such values as "cooperation and co-prosperity" and "community of shared destiny." Besides the economic and political aspects, it emphasises also the cultural facet of China's New Road project as implementing the ideas of China's soft political power, enhancing China's international attractiveness and cultural exchange and helping reduce Chinese deficit in this exchange. Atul Aneja observes that, "by leveraging culture, the Chinese wish to message to the world that the One Belt One Road (OBOR) connectivity project, championed by President Xi Jinping, is an extension of China's symbiotic and peaceful engagement of Asia and Europe that ran for over a millennia [sic] along the Silk Road super-highway."

Aneja, Atul; China
Glaser, Bonnie S.; Melissa E. Murphy; Soft
Hu, Jian; China's
Hu, Jintao; Full
Liu, Yunshan; Hold
Ni, Peimin; Underlying
Wang, Huning; Culture
Wen, Jiabao; Our

3.11 Dialogue

Dialogue is evoked many times by many people. The UNESCO Silk Road website tells us that the history of the old Silk Road is a "history of mutual exchange and dialogue." The key document *Vision* issued by the National Development and Reforms Commission insists that the New Silk Road project it envisages "supports dialogues among different civilizations on the principles of seeking common ground while shelving differences and drawing on each other's strengths, so that all countries can coexist in peace for common prosperity." Yet, Ahmad Talmiz, an Indian diplomat, observes in his discussion of China's new initiative: "Officially, India has focused on the absence of consultation from the Chinese side" and cites an official address India's Foreign Minister Sushma Swaraj delivered in New Delhi on 2 March, 2015.

NDRC; Vision
Talmiz, Ahmed; Who
UNESCO; The UNESCO Silk

3.12 Diversity

The *Vision* states that the New Road project aims to promote "cultural diversity" of countries and "dialogues among different civilizations on the principles of seeking common ground while shelving differences." Bonnie Glaser and Melissa Murphy write about "harmony but difference [*he er butong*]" as the core of the CPC concept. Agatha Kratz quotes Jun Wang, who states that "the AIIB's founding members are very different from each other, in terms of development, values, faiths, and overall expectations. Therefore, China will have to 'find common ground despite differences' (求同存异, *qiutongcunyi*)." Yinhong Shi emphasises that "people are fully entitled to travel on their own roads respectively according to their own practice, experience, and decisions."

Glaser, Bonnie S.; Melissa E. Murphy; Soft
Kratz, Agatha; China's
NDRC; Vision
Shi, Yinhong; The Roles
Zhao, Minghao; China's

3.13 East and West

East and West are two major directions of the Silk Road, which are often evoked in its descriptions, sometimes serving as its synonym. When Aleksander Vučić defines Serbia as "a bridge between East and West," he means the Road in its new form. To Archil Gegeshidze, the New Road means "new relationships between the East and West." And when Binali Yildrim speaks of "a route linking western and eastern civilizations," he refers to the Old and the New Roads. Similarly, in the *Vision*, both the Old and the New Roads "symbolize communication and cooperation between the East and the West." However, the Road does not always refer to this coupling. To Korea's Silk Road Foundation, it connotes just one direction, with the old

Silk Road integrating the East. In Chinese Chengdu, the Road (referred to as Southern here) led to Burma, India and Vietnam. In Kashgar, merchants and traders arriving from the East could choose three directions of further journeys: southward – following the route today covered by the Karakoram Highway, running via the Khunjerab Pass to Islamabad and, further, to India; westward – via the Altai's Erkeshtam Pass (Irkeshtam, Эркеч-Там, 伊尔克什坦) on the border with Kyrgyzstan and, on, along the present-day A371 across Tajikistan to Afghanistan and Iran; and northward – via the Torugart Pass in the Tian Shan Mountains at the border with Kyrgyzstan, Bishkek, present-day Kazakh Shymkent and, further north, towards Siberia. If we add to this the "21st-Century Maritime Silk Road," proposed by Jinping Xi in Indonesia's Jakarta in 2013, it will turn out that, in China, the Silk Road comprises four directions of the world as viewed from the Middle Kingdom (*Zhōngguó*, 中国).

Caravanistan; Irkeshtam
Daily News; Marmaray
Gegeshidze, Archil; The New
Liu, Jing; The ancient
NDRC; Vision
Serbia Construction; Chinese
Silk Road Foundation
Travel China Guide; Southern

3.14 Economic Development

Nadège Rolland observes that the major aim of Jinping Xi's policies is to make China an economic power. The New Road and "the OBOR can help keep China's economic boom alive," insists Zhao Minghao. The project is supposed to help develop west China, which is currently less involved in the country's overall development. Dominique Patton writes about plans to create one million jobs in textile industry in the Xinjiang Uyghur Autonomous Region by 2023, and Camille Brugier explains that the new produce is to be exported to Central Asia. The project is supposed to secure international contracts for Chinese companies and, consequently, help tap on their potential and boost Chinese employment rates. Jinping Xi calls his project the "Silk Road Economic Belt," highlighting the initiative's commercial impact, which is to foster economic growth in the participating countries. With this in mind, he said in his address in Astana that "this will be a great undertaking benefitting the people of all countries along the route." Bruce Pannier argues that Chinese investments in Central Asia will be more advantageous to Chinese companies than to the local ones. Yinhong Shi explains that "economic growth" is one of the four modern international core values. In many countries, the New Silk Road is perceived as an opportunity to enhance their economic development, which is why many observers believe that the Chinese initiative contributes to China's image as a friendly country. Others emphasise the project's global character. According to Justin Lin, it will make China the engine of the global development while Afshini Molavi insists that it will transform the global economy.

Brugier, Camille; China's
Fallon, Theresa; The New
Leer, Yeroen van der; Joshua Yau; China's
Lin, Justin; China's
Molavi, Afshin; Five
NDRC; Vision
Pannier, Bruce; How
Patton, Dominique; Xinjiang
Rolland, Nadège; China's
Shi, Yinhong; The Roles
Xi, Jinping; Speech at Nazarbayev
Zhao, Minghao; China's

3.15 Energy

Energy production and electric power feature as a goal in multiple projects. CASA-1000 is a project involving the European Union and aimed to supply energy from the hydropower plants of Kyrgyzstan and Tajikistan to Afghanistan and Pakistan. The seaport of Gwadar and the corridor which will link it to China are supposed to transport crude oil and natural gas to China, bypassing the Strait of Malacca, i.e. the currently used, but longer and less safe shipping lane. The American concept of the Silk Road presented by Hillary Clinton, which focused on rebuilding Afghanistan's war-devastated economy, referred to the TAPI project, i.e. a pipeline to carry Turkmenistan's gas to Afghanistan, Pakistan and India. Energy and its raw materials clearly connote economic gains, yet, for China, they connote national security as well. Also, they can have a political and social relevance when the respective projects seek to improve the population's quality of life or to advance peaceable international relations, which is what the EU- or US-supported projects seek to accomplish.

Fedorenko, Vladimir; The New
Raza, Syed Irfan; China
U.S. Department of State; New

3.16 Equality

Jurij Tawrowski (Юрий Тавровский) of the Peoples' Friendship University of Russia in Moscow observes: "At the meetings in Ufa, Beijing, Moscow, Durban and New Delhi, the foundations of the new world order have been built brick by brick without envisaging any country's or group of countries' control." He adds that the international relations which are being built today are "horizontal rather than vertical." This means that they are founded on the equality of all the countries involved, rather than on their hierarchy. Peimin Ni of the University of South California quotes Tawrowski and, building on his idea, points out that, unlike in the past, the new relations do not form a pyramid of hierarchical economic and military power. Instead, they are multilateral as decisions follow from agreements among various countries.

Ni, Peimin; The Underlying
Тавровский, Юрий; Новые

3.17 Eurasia

The term Eurasia in the name of the Eurasian Economic Union designates Russia and other countries which were once part of the Soviet Union. Eurasian integration is one of the basic principles articulated in the EEU Treaty. In its *Vision*, China's National Development and Reforms Commission refers to both continents, treating them, in fact, as one geographical continent. Eurasia features also in texts concerning the old and new Silk Roads. Theresa Fallon writes about Jinping Xi's "Grand Strategy for Eurasia." When Zbigniew Brzeziński insisted that "Eurasia is the world's axial supercontinent," the term denoted a key area for the entire world, boasting, as the author listed, 75% of the world's population, 75% of the world's energy resources and 60% of global product. This reasoning builds on the concept proposed by Halford John Mackinder and developed by other authors, in which Eurasia – or, precisely, its variously understood central part – is crucial to the world and its history.

Brzeziński, Zbigniew; A Geostrategy
Fallon, Theresa; The New
Mackinder, Halford John; The Geographical
NDRC; Vision

3.18 Exchange

Freight transport is a reason why many commentators often write about trade in goods, as does Pierre-Louis Caron in the title of his "China Gets French Wine in Exchange for Chemicals." The *Vision* mentions exchange between parliaments, cities, NGOs, people and civilisations; it also mentions academic exchange, information exchange and cultural exchange. UNESCO's Silk Road online platform tells us that along the old Road people also traded in goods and exchanged ideas. Junjie Ma explains that, like in the past, the Silk Road is a "market for ideas" today and, in this context, he refers to Ronald Coase's book. Like in the past again, the economic exchange makes the Road now a formative factor in the division of labour among countries, regions and cities. Junjie Ma writes that while the Road once "helped introduce Buddhism and Islam to China," now "the hope here is that with the One Belt, One Road strategy, a much bigger and more complex market for ideas will emerge." He inquires whether this market will make China open up more. Or, perhaps, Europe and the West should be asked whether *they* will open up more.

Caron, Pierre-Louis; China
Coase, Ronald; The Market
Ma, Junjie; The new
NDRC; Vision
UNESCO; The UNESCO Silk

3.19 Friendship

The *Vision* states that the project aims to foster not only "peace and friendship" among the countries along the Road but also "peace and friendship among people of all countries." Jinping Xi tellingly titled the speech he delivered in Astana in 2013 "Promote People-to-People Friendship and Create a Better Future." The *People's Daily* (人民日报), the official newspaper of the CPC, has set up a New Silk Road information platform "aiming at promoting (…) friendly relationships between China and other Silk Road countries." Yeroen van der Leer and Joshua Yau (and many others) observe that the new initiative is supposed to build friendly relations among the many countries neighbouring China.

NDRC; Vision
People's Daily; Of the
Xi, Jinping; Speech at Nazarbayev

3.20 Gateway

Many places turn out to be gateways to many other places. Writing about the port of Piraeus, Liz Alderman states that it has become China's gateway to Europe. To Bogdan Możdżyński, it is Lodz and its railway station that serve as a gateway to Europe. And during a meeting with Jinping Xi at the summit of the Shanghai Cooperation Organisation in Tashkent on 24 June, 2016, President of Belarus Aleksandr Lukashenko told the БЕЛТА agency that his country was "ready to become 'a western gate' for this organization." To Adedan Ashebir of the SACE Foundation, the OBOR has made Kenya and its capital Nairobi "Africa's gateway for business, investment and trade." Being a gateway entails therefore both benefitting economically from mediation in goods exchange and enjoying an increased prestige, relevance and significance a place, or a country, gains in the network of international relations of the Silk New World.

Alderman, Liz; Port
Możdżyński, Bogdan; Chiński
SACE Foundation
БЕЛТА; Belarus

3.21 Globality

References to globality surface once and again. For example, the Dubai International Financial Centre states that its aim is to "contribute to Dubai's reputation as a global business hub." The notion of the global often appears in the context of the Chinese New Silk Road proposal. The *Vision* explains: "It is a great undertaking that will benefit people around the world." Nadège Rolland concludes: "The birth of a transcontinental economic corridor, as envisioned by the Chinese authorities, could change the global landscape, shifting the focus of strategy and commerce to the Eurasian landmass from the waters surrounding it and reducing the significance of U.S. naval supremacy." Yeroen van der Leer and Joshua Yau observe that the project logically follows from the "go global" strategy China has been implementing since 2001 to increase its foreign investments. Bonnie Glaser and Melissa Murphy add that the Five-Year Plan for Cultural Development, adopted in 2006, implemented the "go global" strategy in culture, aiming to "expand Chinese culture's coverage and international impact." This entails exporting not only the Chinese capital but also Chinese ideas, values and norms. In a debate on the role of China in the world, Yinhong Shi argued that "what is best for China is not necessarily best for any of the others," and Justin Yifu Lin explained that China's joining the world's biggest economies meant "more responsibility – and assert[ed] more influence – on the global stage." Helga Zepp-LaRouche said that China's latest project "is not only capable of bringing people together economically, but also of enhancing cultural and other exchanges among peoples, becoming a completely new concept of peace order of the 21st century." Mahdi Darius Nazemroaya observes that the convergence of the Chinese New Silk Road project, Russia's Eurasian Economic Union project and other concepts developed by cooperating countries heralds the rise of a new "Silk World Order." Mathias Mertens states that "talk of a New Silk Road can be heard in all corners of the world." Let us add that, in fact, quite different things can be heard in this talk.

Cohen, David; China's
Glaser, Bonnie S.; Melissa E. Murphy; Soft
Leer, Yeroen van der; Joshua Yau; China's
Lin, Justin Yifu; China's
Mertens, Matthias; Along
NDRC; Vision
Nazemroaya, Mahdi Darius; The Silk
New Silk Road Company Ltd.
China Copyright and Media; Outline of the National
Shi, Yinhong; The Roles
Zepp-LaRouche, Helga; The New Silk Road Will

3.22 Harmony

The *Vision* states that the Chinese initiative aims to help people and communities along the Silk Road "live in harmony, peace and prosperity." Discussing the origins of the notion of harmony, Michael Billington and Peimin Ni look back to *datong* (大同), i.e. the concept of Great Harmony or Great Unity attributed to Confucius (551 – 479 BC). Bonnie Glaser and Melissa Murphy relate that, according to some Chinese authors, harmony and other categories used in the Chinese document are universal and can complement, rather than replace, the American values, which now prevail in international politics. Other Chinese researchers point out that "the concepts of harmonious society and harmonious world could provide an alternative to Western values." Glaser and Murphy explain that the harmony of society and the world implies, for example, a balance between the economic development and social well-being and conclude that the building of a harmonious society can make such model "a powerful attraction and inspiration not only to the Chinese people, but to the people throughout the world." Changping Fang observes that the international attractiveness of the idea of "harmonious society and world" can contribute to increasing China's soft power in international relations, i.e. to China's greater authority, prestige and, related, opportunities of global influence. Angang Hu, Professor at the University of Qinghua, believes that the Chinese idea of harmonious social development is "more influential and alluring than American democracy and human rights." The worldwide dissemination of harmony as a "valuable idea of Chinese culture" is an aim of, for example, The Silk Road International Arts Festival in Xi'an. To conclude, let us add that, in Vladimir Putin's view, China's One Belt One Road project and Russia's Eurasian Economic Union project "complement each other very harmoniously."

Billington, Michael; Xi
Fang, Changping; Comparison; qtd. in Glaser, Bonnie S.; Melissa E. Murphy; Soft
Glaser, Bonnie S.; Melissa E. Murphy; Soft
Hu, Angang; Build; qtd. in Glaser, Bonnie S.; Melissa E. Murphy; Soft
NDRC; Vision
Ni, Peimin; The Underlying
President of Russia; Press

3.23 Hegemony

Marcin Kaczmarski explains that, "as the idea of Sinocentrism has it, China regards itself as the only central, supreme and sovereign agent that often enjoys the right to determine the policies and politics of its neighbours and near-neighbours." Indian diplomat Ahmad Talmiz observes: "India shares the view of several countries in Northeast and Southeast Asia that far from being an enterprise founded on wide and substantial cooperation, the OBOR could in fact be the vehicle for China's influence, if not hegemony, across Asia." He adds that if China's initial proposals "seemed to be China-centric, the principal focus of present-day comment by Chinese writers is on the need for participating countries to work closely together." Piotr Winnicki gave his study a subtitle that pithily depicts China's new project: *Droga do budowania imperium* [Towards building an empire]. Nadège Rolland highlights the economic aspect of the Chinese initiative, which aims to "integrate China's neighbors more closely with the Chinese economy, enmeshing them in a network of trade ties, transportation links, and multilateral regional institutions that will have China at their center, enhancing Beijing's influence over the weaker, poorer nations that surround it."

Kaczmarski, Marcin; Jedwabna
Rolland, Nadège; China's
Talmiz, Ahmad; Who's
Winnicki, Piotr; Nowy

3.24 History

Theresa Fallon discusses the history of the term Silk Road, which was used first by Ferdinand von Richthofen as *Seidenstraße* in 1877. She also examines the much shorter history of the New Silk Road, which had been a US concept before it was picked up by the PRC and other countries. Yeroen van der Leer and Joshua Yau, in turn, envisage a future history. An important stage in the implementation of Chinese initiatives is scheduled to be completed by 2049, marking the centenary of the People's Republic of China. Melissa Murphy and Bonnie Glaser, citing Yugang Cheng, write that "China's ancient history and traditional culture are viewed by most scholars as a valuable source of soft power for attracting not only East Asian neighbors with whom China shares a Confucian heritage but also the wider international community." Since the history of the Silk Road itself is relevant and precious, it is often referenced in a variety of contexts. The *Vision* states that "for thousands of years, the Silk Road Spirit – 'peace and cooperation, openness and inclusiveness, mutual learning and mutual benefit' – has been passed from generation to generation, promoted the progress of human civilization." At the opening ceremony of the Marmaray Tunnel, Turkey's Minister of Transport Binali Yildrim said that the Tunnel was "a continuation of the historical Silk Road." The international initiative of the Transport Corridor Europe-Caucasus-Asia (TRACECA) tends to be referred to as "The Silk Road of the 21st century," which is an allusion to the old Silk Road and its history. And when an array of tourist agencies – such as the Silk Road Railway – advertise their trips, they also evoke the ancient times and legendary associations. History features, too, in India's Mausam Project, which Akhilesh Pillalamarri depicts as follows: "India is using its history, culture and geography to compete with China's 'Maritime Silk Road.'" The Treaty of the Eurasian Economic Union lists respect for history of its member states among its fundamental principles.

Cheng, Yugang; Build
Daily News; Marmaray
Fallon, Theresa; The New
Glaser, Bonnie S.; Melissa E. Murphy; Soft
Leer, Yeroen van der; Joshua Yau; China's
NDRC; Vision
Pillalamarri, Akhilesh; Project
Silk Road Railway
Waugh, Daniel; Richthofen's

3.25 Independence

The principle of "not influencing other countries' domestic politics" has been part of China's international policies since the mid-20th century. The *Vision* explains that China's new initiative complies with the five principles of the UN Charter, one of which is "mutual non-interference in each other's internal affairs." Writing about the New Silk Road, Helga Zepp-LaRouche observes: "This also signifies a new model of cooperation among the nations of the world. (...) they must nonetheless respect the different levels of development, history, culture, and social systems, and above all, respect national sovereignty."

Banerjee, Dipankar; China's
NDRC; Vision
Zepp-LaRouche, Helga; The New Silk Road Will
Zepp-LaRouche, Helga; The New Silk Road leads

3.26 Influence

Ahmad Talmiz states that "the OBOR could in fact be the vehicle for China's influence, if not hegemony, across Asia." In a similar vein, Marcin Kaczmarski observes that the New Road is supposed to "underpin the expansion of China's political influence," but he adds that "it is an open political project without clearly delineated boundaries." As such, the New Road can serve as an instrument of influence outside Asia as well. According to David Dollar, the Chinese New Road affects various parts of Asia, Africa and Europe while China is becoming a global superpower. Some commentators consider it a result of infrastructure development whereas others attribute it to China's "soft power" of ideas and values. As early as in 2006, Angang Hu insisted that the Chinese ideal of harmonious society was "more influential and alluring than American democracy and human rights." On this model, China's impact on the world is predicated on the global attractiveness of values and ideas associated with the new initiative.

Dollar, David; China's
Glaser, Bonnie S.; Melissa E. Murphy; Soft
Kaczmarski, Marcin; Nowy
Talmiz, Ahmad; Who's

3.27 Infrastructure

Michael Billington observes that China's project of the New Silk Road entails the "greatest burst in infrastructure development on a global scale in history." François Godement calculates that this will consume over $300 billion invested by China and $890 billion provided by the China Development Bank. Infrastructure is crucial to several projects planned and launched by various countries. In the Chinese project, infrastructure is so important that Piotr Winnicki assesses that it involves "the construction and modernisation of transport infrastructure – railways, roads, inland ports, seaports, airports, oil and gas pipelines and telecommunications networks." Infrastructure is also central to other Silk Road projects even though they are less comprehensive than China's programme. The US concept focuses on the rebuilding of Afghanistan's infrastructure by constructing pipelines, bridges, highways, hydroelectric power plants and power lines. Turkey seeks to develop rail and road transportation. India wants to build seaports and highways while Georgia and other Caucasus countries prioritise the development of communications in which railways, maritime transport and pipelines are combined. Rail connections are important in Russia's Eurasian Economic Union project. Everywhere, infrastructure has also other – political, economic, social, cultural and environmental – facets to it, though their proportions and appraisal may differ locally. Established by the PRC, the Silk Road Fund plans to invest $40 billion in infrastructure enterprises. Nadège Rolland calls it "China's infrastructure diplomacy."

Asian Development Bank; The New
Billington, Michael; Xi
Eurasian Econiomic Union
Fedorenko, Vladimir; The New
Godement, François; Introduction
Rolland, Nadège; China's
The Hans India; What
Winnicki, Piotr; Nowy
Xinhuanet; Silk Road

3.28 Integration

During his foreign trips in 2008–13, China's Premier Keqiang Li promoted the policy of building "a new corridor of interconnectivity." Paul Vandenberg and Khan Kikkawa analyse the economic consequences of the Chinese project in terms of integrating local enterprises into "global value chains," which bring economic benefits. Still, the *Vision* describes a further-ranging integration of markets, finances and countries. Speaking at the University of Astana in 2013, Jinping Xi said that the project was exactly what the Silk Road countries needed "to make the[ir] economic ties closer, mutual cooperation deeper." This is how Tim Summers explains the President's statements: "Xi has talked about connectivity in terms of trade, investment, finance, and flows of tourists and students." Integration is an important factor also in the projects championed by India, such as Mausam and connections to Central Asia's highways via the seaports of Iran, which both involve communication, economic and political integration. To the Eurasian Economic Union, infrastructure integration is of economic and political significance as well, the difference being that India's projects are geared to India's benefits while Russia's initiatives cater to Russia's interests. Indian diplomat Ahmad Talmiz claims that both China and India "accept the importance of expanding connectivities in Asia." And Vladimir Putin addressing the UN General Assembly in 2015 spoke about the possibilities of and needs for "integration of integrations," i.e. fusing various countries' integration ideas into one. Jurij Kulincew (Юрий Кулинцев) writes that the Chinese project "is not China's solo but a symphony performed by all the interested countries." Mahdi Darius Nazemroaya gives the idea a slightly different wording: "Interconnectedness is the name of the game," and emphasises the global nature of China's enterprises: "They are about a Silk World that includes every corner of the planet. (...) The Chinese are looking at major projects to help connect Latin American countries with one another and with Eurasia. One of these ventures is a massive railroad project to connect Brazil with the Pacific ports of Peru."

NDRC; Vision
Nazemroaya, Mahdi Darius; Neither
Putin, Wladymir; U.N.
Summers, Tim; What
Szczudlik-Tatar, Justyna; China's
Talmiz, Ahmad; Who's
Vandenberg, Paul; Khan Kikkawa; Global
Xi, Jinping; Speech at Nazarbayev
Кулинцев, Юрий; Один

3.29 Money

Money is addressed when costs are compared, for example, when Thomas Puls estimates that railway transport is five times and air transport eleven times as expensive as maritime transport. François Godement calculates that China intends to spend $300 billion on the Road project and the China Development Bank another $890 billion. Money is mentioned in descriptions of various institutions, with the Silk Road Fund and its $40 billion capital topping the list. Money is also implicitly referenced when politicians, business people, journalists and experts discuss financial profits, as in the title "Jedwabny Szlak. Eksperci: Polska może na tym dobrze zarobić" [Silk Road: Experts say Poland can earn well on It]. In an interview with Gilly Wright, Cheng of the Bank of China states that the New Road will be "a platform to drive international usage of renminbi" since the currency is used in various parts of the Road and, starting in October 2016, it became the official currency of the International Monetary Fund.

Godement, François; Introduction
Polskie Radio.pl; Jedwabny
Puls, Thomas; China's
Wright, Gilly; New Silk
Xinhuanet; Silk

3.30 Multicentricity

Commenting on China's proposals, Indian diplomat Ahmad Talmiz underscores that "a multi-polar Asia already exists and India is an important part of it." However, the project is not only about Asia. The *Vision* presents the initiative of building the new Road as "embracing the trend towards a multipolar world." Mahdi Darius Nazemroaya writes that the project moulds a "multipolar Silk World Order." Drawing on Jurij Tawrowski, Peimin Ni observes that "the new world order is multilateral" and cites as an example the Asian Infrastructure Investment Bank (AIIB), where no member has a right of veto, unlike in the World Bank and the International Monetary Fund, where such right is enjoyed only by the US. With this in mind, Minghao Zhao explains: "The AIIB embodies China's desire to practice multilateralism in international finance." Multicentricity and multilaterality are interconnected. Multicentricity, i.e. a lack of one centre of the world order, means that the world order is co-formed by several countries in multilateral agreements. This is the reason why the *Vision* envisages multilateral finances, trade, communications channels and interests.

NDRC; Vision
Nazemroaya, Mahdi Darius; Neither
Ni, Peimin; Underlying
Talmiz, Ahmad; Who's
Zhao, Minghao; China's
Тавровский, Юрий; Новые

3.31 Multiplicity

According to the *Vision*, the New Road "is a pluralistic and open process" because it accomodates multiple participants and multiple flexible initiatives which can be implemented in multiple ways. Jurij Kulincew writes that this "is not China's solo but a symphony performed by all the interested countries." Helga Zepp-LaRouche points out that the Chinese initiative provides "a new model of cooperation among the nations of the world. (…) they must nonetheless respect the different levels of development, history, culture, and social systems, and above all, respect national sovereignty. That is Cusa's idea of unity in multiplicity, and it must be inspired by a tender love for the idea of the community of nations."

NDRC; Vision
Zepp-LaRouche, Helga; The New Silk Road Leads
Кулинцев, Юрий; Один

3.32 Natural resources

Vladimir Fedorenko explains that natural resources are crucial to various projects. The American Silk Road focuses on Turkmenistan's natural gas for Afghanistan, Pakistan and India. The Chinese project also targets Turkmenistan's gas and oil, but transported via Uzbekistan and Kazakhstan to China. The 2004 agreement between Lukoil and Uzbekneftegaz, funded by the Asian Development Bank, the Islamic Development Bank and the Korean Development Bank, concerns Uzbekistan's gas for Russia. The Asian Development Bank writes about gas and oil in Azerbaijan, Kazakhstan, Uzbekistan and Turkmenistan; copper in Uzbekistan and Mongolia; gold in Mongolia, Uzbekistan and Tajikistan; and Uzbekistan's uranium, Turkmenistan's rare metals and Tajikistan's silver and antimony. According to Yeroen van der Leer and Joshua Yau, the New Road is supposed to give China "long-term access to natural resources," which the country must import. This strategy is exemplified in the project of copper mining in Kazakhstan adopted by China Nonferrous Metal Mining and the interest of China's Silk Road Found in gold mining.

Asian Development Bank; The New
China Daily; Chinese
China Nonferrous
Fedorenko, Vladimir; The New
Leer, Yeroen van der; Joshua Yau; China's

3.33 Node

The New Road, like the old one, is a network or roads, projects and enterprises, which is why communication junctions, nodes and centres are highly relevant to it. This is where various roads and initiatives intersect. As Wade Shephard sees it, it is the port of Baku, Azerbaijan, that finds itself "at the new crossroads of Eurasia." In turn, the Dubai International Finance Center is "a global financial centre strategically located between the East and West." According to Adedan Ashebir from Kenya, the Chinese project "will help the country to become a regional trade hub and entry point for direct foreign investment."

> Four Seasons Hotel Dubai
> Levchenko, Anastasia; Kenya
> Shepard, Wade; An Inside

3.34 Openness

The *Vision* mentions openness on thirty-nine occasions. First, it presents openness as consistently intrinsic to the old Road, which everybody could participate in. Further, it states that the New Road is to display even greater openness: "The Initiative is open for cooperation. It covers, but is not limited to, the area of the ancient Silk Road. It is open to all countries." The document's separate chapter is devoted to opening China's regions, in particular central and western ones, to the world. It also speaks of open trade and building a quick transport corridor connecting Beijing to Moscow, dubbing it "key windows opening to the North." Speaking in Jakarta in 2013, Jinping Xi listed openness among the five chief principles of the Chinese initiative. China's Consul General to Petersburg Yan Chi Ji (Яньчи Цзи) explains: "We are always ready to work with any and every country of our planet and with our American partners." Michael Billington calls the Road a huge infrastructure project beneficial to all humanity and offering cooperation to all. Justin Yifu Lin in his discussion of the industrialisation of Africa, related to the Road project, observes that it is "good for all." Yi Wang adds that "the OBOR is based on 'open cooperation' (开放合作, *kaifang hezuo*)" as opposed to the US Marshall Plan, to which it is sometimes compared. When Marcin Kaczmarski concludes that "the plan is 'doomed to succeed' first of all due to its indefinite aims and open character," he means that the plan is flexible and receptive to new initiatives.

Billington, Michael; Xi
HKTDC; What
Kaczmarski, Marcin; Nowy
Lin, Justin Yifu; Industry
Ministry of Foreign Affairs; Foreign Minister; qtd. in Bondaz, Antoine; Rebalancing
NDRC; Vision
Цзи, Яньчи, Это

3.35 Partnership

In *The New Silk Road*, the Asian Development Bank stresses that "the spirit of trust and confidence (…) among good neighbors and good partners has led to better prospects for all." The *Vision* insists that the project establishes and consolidates partnership among the New Road countries. When Jurij Tawrowski (Юрий Тавровский) writes that the new world order emerging from the project is, "not vertical, but horizontal," Peimin Ni explains that it means that this new order is based on partnership rather than on leadership.

Asian Development Bank; The New
NDRC; Vision
Ni, Peimin; The Underlying
Тавровский, Юрий; Новые

3.36 Peace

In 2011, the Asian Development Bank presented its programme for Central Asia, emphasising the "spirit of security and trust." In 2013, Istanbul hosted The International Silk Road Congress *Rethinking the Road of Trade, Cooperation and Peace*. The *Vision* refers to the Five Principles of Peaceful Coexistence of the UN Charter. Indian general Dipankar Banerjee stresses that these principles were "jointly propagated by Jawaharlal Nehru and Zhou Enlai in 1954" – India's and China's first Prime Ministers. In his description of the principles of the New Road, Qingguo Jia lists the "peaceful rise (和平崛起, *heping jueqi*)" of China's international relevance, and Yesui Zhang, China's Vice-Minister of Foreign Affairs, insists that the OBOR is "not directed against any specific country or organisation (不针对任何国家

或特定的组织, *bu zhendui renhe guojia huo teding zuzhi*)." Jurij Kulincew (Юрий Кулинцев) of the Russian Academy of Sciences writes that the New Road can contribute to "universal peace on the planet," and Nake Kamrany of the University of South California discusses "China's New World Order for global peace and prosperity." Helga Zepp-LaRouche of the Schiller Institute describes the Chinese project as "a completely new concept of peace order of the 21st century." In Xi'an, The Silk Road International Arts Festival is organised to promote peace as "a valuable idea of Chinese culture" all over the world. Theresa Fallon, nevertheless, cites another military pundit, Admiral Jianguo Sun, Chief of Staff of Chinese People's Liberation Army, who said: "'No confrontation, no conflict' does not mean 'no struggle'(…) without the struggle the United States would still have no respect for China's core interests."

Asian Development Bank; The New
Banerjee, Dipankar; China's
Fallon, Theresa; The New
INOMISC; International
Jia, Qingguo; One Belt; qtd. in: Cohen, David; China's
Kamrany, Nake M.; China's
NDRC; Vision
Zepp-LaRouche, Helga; The New Silk Road Will
Zhang, Yesui; 'The One; qtd. in: Bondaz, Antoine; Rebalancing
Кулинцев, Юрий; Один

3.37 People

The UNESCO Silk Road established in 1988 explains: "The term 'Silk Roads' refers to a vast network of land and maritime trade and communication routes (…). The incessant movement of peoples and goods along these routes resulted in an unprecedented transmission and exchange of knowledge, ideas, beliefs, customs and traditions over three millennia." Given this, UNESCO's "online platform continues the Silk Road's tradition and facilitates dialogue, encounters and exchanges among authorities, scholars, artists, educators, tourism professionals, students and youth." Founded in 2005, the Seoul-based Silk Road Foundation sets itself goals which also revisit the past: "The Silk Road had been a passageway and a square that connected people in the ancient times." The Foundation states that its mission is to facilitate contacts and communication among people from various countries. When presenting the New Silk Road project in Astana in 2013, Jinping Xi titled his speech "Promote People-to-People Friendship and Create a Better Future." The *Vision* insists on disseminating "the spirit of friendly cooperation of the Silk Road by promoting extensive cultural and academic exchanges, personnel exchanges and cooperation, media cooperation, youth and women exchanges and volunteer services." Describing the new project, Jinping Xi states: "This will be a great undertaking benefitting the people of all countries along the route." When Helga Zepp-LaRouche addresses well-being and decent life, she admits: "I think the new Silk Road is exactly what is needed to help people reach that goal." Saying that, she means also the Chinese initiative. Michael Billington states that the New Silk Road involves "projects of benefit to all mankind," and Jurij Kulincew (Юрий Кулинцев) adds: "China is ready to make a greater contribution to the development of the entire humanity." The human dimension of the New Road should therefore involve both human contacts that underpin the enterprise and the benefits it will bring to people in the countries involved in the New Road and, even, to the world's entire population.

Billington, Michael; Xi
NDRC; Vision
Silk Road Foundation
UNESCO; Reviving
Xi, Jinping; Speech at Nazarbayev
Xi, Jinping; Silk
Xi, Jinping; Speech by Chinese
Zepp-LaRouche, Helga; The New Silk Road Will
Кулинцев, Юрий; Один

3.38 Position

Some analysts believe that the new project is to help China achieve a stronger position in Central Asia and counterbalance the influences of Russia and the US. Others, such as Minghao Zhao, point out that "the OBOR is crucial in consolidating China's status as the largest developing country." As early as in 2010, Ye Zicheng explicitly emphasised global aims, concluding that "if China does not become a world power, the rejuvenation of the Chinese nation will be incomplete." Yeroen van der Leer and Joshua Yau explain that the Road project is an implementation of the "going global" strategy China has adopted, yet they add that "there is a long and winding road ahead before China, along with all the underdeveloped nations across Central Asia and the Middle East, can reach the position, influence and level of prosperity that they once held in the days of the ancient silk routes."

Leer, Yeroen van der; Joshua Yau; China's
Szczudlik-Tatar, Justyna; China's
Zhao, Minghao; China's
Zicheng, Ye; Inside; qtd. in: Fallon, Theresa; The New

3.39 Prosperity

The prosperity of all countries involved in the New Silk Road project is emphatically addressed in the *Vision* by the National Development and Reforms Commission of the PRC. In the report for PricewaterhouseCoopers, Yeroen van der Leer and Joshua Yau conclude that the initiative of new land and maritime contacts described in the *Vision* is only germinating and that China has a long and twisting road ahead before it can "reach the position, influence and level of prosperity that [it] once held in the days of the ancient silk routes." Prosperity as related to China's proposal is also addressed by Nake Kamrany, Professor of Economics at the University of Southern California, US, but he focuses not only on the prosperity of China and other countries involved in the project, but also on the prosperity of the entire planet since, in his view, the project will certainly affect it: "It is China's New World Order for global peace and prosperity." The Asian Development Bank also references prosperity as a rationale of its 10-year programme for Central Asia, titled *The New Silk Road*, and calls it "Co-operation for Prosperity." When Helga Zepp-LaRouche put forward her global concept of the "World Land-Bridge" in the 1990s, she also insisted that it aimed to further the prosperity of humanity.

Asian Development Bank; The New
Kamrany, Nake M.; China's
Leer, Yeroen van der; Joshua Yau; China's
NDRC; Vision
The World Land Bridge

3.40 Reciprocity

In Jakarta in 2013, Jinping Xi talked about "work for win-win coopera-tion." The *Vision* insists: "The Belt and Road Initiative is a way for win-win cooperation that promotes common development and prosperity." China's Consul in Petersburg Yan Chi Ji (Яньчи Цзи) relies on a metaphor and refers to one of the Project's three principles to explain the idea: "Shared use – we all bake the cake together and then divide it fairly." Peimin Ni, in turn, provides an explanation based on the Confucian interpretation of the ancient Chinese idea of *tianxia* 天下 – a community of shared destiny of "all under heaven." If we are this community, we have no other op-tion but work together for the common prosperity: "There is no zero-sum game! It is either zero-zero, if we fight against each other, or win-win, if we cooperate!" Thus, if one wins, another cannot possibly lose. And if we believe that our win is coupled with another's loss, we mistakenly call our loss a win. Indian diplomat Ahmad Talmiz observes that if the Chinese New Road project is really implemented on the basis of "the cooperative spirit," it will turn out to genuinely make its declared "win-win" principle a reality and we will all end up as winners.

NDRC; Vision
Ni, Peimin; The Underlying
Talmiz, Ahmad; Who's
Xi, Jinping; Speech by Chinese
Цзи, Яньчи; Это

3.41 Responsibility

In his 2012 study, Yinhong Shi argued: "There should be no doubt in China that she must greatly increase her bearing of international responsi-bility." He added that the insight should result "from the equal consultation between her and the external world, rather than from any 'dictation' or coercion by the latter; and largely [match] the increase of her reasonable international rights and privileges." Drawing on this, Justin Lin wrote four years later: "To join the ranks of the world's high-income economies, China must use markets and resources, both at home and abroad, more efficiently. And it must assume more responsibility – and assert more influence – on the global stage." The Chinese project of building a New Silk Road, or, as some prefer to put it, a Silk New World Order, is a response to and an enactment of the postulates to increase international and global responsibility and opportunities. The *Vision* announces: "China is committed to shouldering more responsibilities and obligations within its capabilities, and making greater contributions to the peace and development of mankind."

Lin, Justin Yifu; China's
NDRC; Vision
Shi, Yinhong; The Roles
Sprengel, Mieczysław; Katarzyna Sprengel; Evaluation

3.42 Roads

Roads can have an economic dimension, significance and value as is made clear by the economist Thomas Puls, who compares the lengths of roads and the times and costs of freight transportation between China and Europe, taking into account transport by land, sea and, even, air. Yet roads can be relevant also in other senses. For example, Georgian diplomat Archil Gegeshidze sees the roads of the old and new Silk Roads as "a multifaceted system of spatio-temporal relationship among nations, states and civilisations, which is the result of an evolutionary process of a co-operation on the enormous Eurasian landmass." And Liqun Jin, President of the AIIB, quotes the Chinese proverb which says: "If you want to develop, build a road."

Gegeshidze, Archil; The New
Kunge, James; How
Puls, Thomas; China's

3.43 Security

Security is a frequently addressed issue. Minghao Zhao writes that the OBOR will contribute to the development of collaboration between the PRC and the European Union in ensuring secure sea navigation and protection against piracy: "Working together with their European counterparts, Chinese naval task forces have escorted more than 5,500 commercial vessels through the pirate-plagued waters of the Gulf of Aden." Justyna Szczudlik-Tatar observes that the pirate threat to the navigation through the Strait of Malacca is one of the reasons behind the Chinese initiative of the New Silk Road. Camille Brugier writes, in turn, that the initiative is supposed to give China energy security by providing access to crude oil and natural gas resources in various regions of Asia and the world. And Yiwei Wang views the entire OBOR project as aimed at "building a community of interests and security between China and its neighbours, including both the US and Japan."

Brugier, Camille; China's, s. 3
Szczudlik-Tatar, Justyna; China's, s. 4
Wang, Yiwei; How, s. 7
Zhao, Minghao; China's, s. 10

3.44 Sharia

The Islamic Development Bank states that its operations are "in accordance with the principles of Sharia, i.e., Islamic Law." Anita Hawser writes: "Traders along the old Silk Road were no doubt familiar with financial contracts based on Islamic principles, and today buyers and sellers along the New Silk Road, joining Asia and the Middle East, are realizing the possibilities. Ernst & Young's Global Islamic Banking Centre predicts that Islamic trade finance will become the preferred choice for rapid-growth markets." Hawser cites also Ghazanfar Naqvi of the Standard Chartered, a London-based international bank: "'We started using murabaha,' explains Naqvi, 'and over the years we have added other instruments.'" Zeti Akhtar Aziz, Governor of the Bank Negara Malaysia, Malaysia's central bank, said at the GIFF Investors & Issuers Forum in Kuala Lumpur on 28 March, 2007: "Islamic finance is well positioned to be a vehicle on the New Silk Road (...). The emergence of the New Silk Road reflects the increasing and evolving economic and financial relationships and inter-linkages, with Islamic finance well positioned to further facilitate these linkages (...). Islamic finance does not only involve the avoidance of riba (usury) but also extends to issues relating to ethical values, such as fair trade and environmental protection." Let us add that, in the Quran, *ribā* designates unfair profit from such dealings as usury.

Aziz, Zeti Akhtar; Islamic
Hawser, Anita; Islamic
Islamic Development Bank

3.45 Silk Road

Statements and declarations about the New Silk Road often refer to the old Road and the meanings and values attributed to the old Road tend to be transposed onto the New one. The old Road is often referred to in terms of the prosperity and affluence of China and other Silk Road counties. Commercial exchange went hand in hand with cultural exchange as the caravans carried goods along with religions, languages, political ideas, artistic styles and craft expertise. Vladimir Fedorenko adds: "The significance of the historic Silk Road lies in its unique nature – no authority or government could ever claim a monopoly on creation and control of the Silk Road." When Irene Cheng concludes that, to Eduard Shevardnadze, the Great Silk Road was a "route of tolerance (…). This route will serve for the movements of men, ideas, and Gods," she refers to both the old and the new Roads. The Chinese *Vision* (2015), declares: "For thousands of years, the Silk Road Spirit – 'peace and cooperation, openness and inclusiveness, mutual learning and mutual benefit' – has been passed from generation to generation, promoted the progress of human civilization, and contributed greatly to the prosperity and development of the countries along the Silk Road." For the sake of comparison, here is what Haruhiko Kuroda, President of the Asian Development Bank, said in 2011: "The spirit of trust and confidence that has evolved through the years among good neighbors and good partners has led to better prospects for all." The values and meanings ascribed to the old Road are essential in the contemporary context, for they are supposed to legitimise the New Road initiatives. The old and the new Roads are peculiarly interdependent and mutually affect each other's presumed meanings and values. New initiatives clothe themselves in the traditional meanings and values while the past is reinterpreted to correspond to the new contexts, actions, aims and needs. The travel agency Silk Road Railway advertises its flagship trip by embellishing it with the wonders of the Silk Road: genial hospitality, magnificent monuments, outstanding architecture, legendary treasures and the breath-taking sights of cities and deserts. The Silk Road seems to have a less instrumental and more autotelic value to the Silk Road Foundation, which was established "to promote the study and preservation of cultures and art on Inner Asia and the Silk Road."

Asian Development Bank; The New
Cheng, Irene; The New

Fedorenko, Vladimir; The New, s. 3
NDRC; Vision
Silk Road Foundation
Silk Road Railway
Waugh, Daniel C.; The Silk

3.46 Socialism

Bonnie Glaser and Melissa Murphy remind that "president Jiang Zemin announced the decision on building socialist 'spiritual civilization' at the 15th CPC Congress in 1998. (…)

For the CPC, it has reinforced the importance of building a socialist core value system that can strengthen 'the cohesiveness of the Chinese nation.'" Glaser and Murphy highlight "attention to solving social welfare issues and putting the 'people first.'" They also believe that it is possible that "Beijing will promote Chinese socialist values as an alternative to Western values." At the 18th CPC Congress in 2012, Jintao Hu explained: "Core socialist values are the soul of the Chinese nation and serve as the guide for building socialism with Chinese characteristics." He listed prosperity, social justice, democracy, equality and friendship and spoke about efforts to build harmonious socialist society. John Wong concludes that, relying on the New Road as a tool, Jinping Xi seeks to make China a "socialist cultural superpower."

Glaser, Bonnie S.; Melissa E. Murphy; Soft
Hu Jintao's report
Wong, John; China's

3.47 Soft power

Atul Aneja describes China's soft power developed along the Silk Road. Bonnie Glaser and Melissa Murphy cite Joseph Nye to explain China's distinct notion of soft power ensuing form ideas and moral values. They highlight the Confucian legacy of soft power, in which moral strength is considered superior to physical prowess while it is believed that "the kingly way [*wang dao*] will triumph over the hegemon's way [*ba dao*]." The Chinese initiative of rebuilding the old or building the New Silk Road seems to be part of "China's smile diplomacy," discussed, for example, by Brad Glosserman and Katarzyna and Mieczysław Sprengel.

Aneja, Atul; China
Glaser, Bonnie S.; Melissa E. Murphy; Soft
Glosserman, Brad; China's
Nye, Joseph S.; The Rise
Sprengel, Mieczysław; Katarzyna Sprengel; Evaluation

3.48 Time

The time of travel has its calculated worth and distinct significance also in new Silk Roads. With this in mind, Thomas Puls estimates and compares the time it takes to transport cargo between Europe and China: 1–3 days by air, 19–23 days by rail and 30–36 by sea. Of course, in this case, the sooner the better, but also the more expensive, for rail transport turns out to be five times and air transport eleven times as expensive as sea shipping.

Puls, Thomas; China's

3.49 Tolerance

Irena Cheng writes that Eduard Shevardnadze viewed the Great Silk Road not only in terms of the economy but also as a "route of tolerance." The *Vision* insists that the new project "advocates tolerance among civilizations, respects the paths and modes of development chosen by different countries."

Cheng, Irene; The New
NDRC; Vision

3.50 Tourism

In his analysis of the projects involving Central Asia, Vladimir Fedorenko observes that "important yet underdeveloped sector concerning all Central Asian states is tourism." The goal of tourism development is articulated in the *Vision* in the section devoted to human contacts: "We should enhance cooperation in and expand the scale of tourism." Tourists already use the Trans-Siberian Railway, the Tashkent-Samarkand high-speed rail line and an array of arrangements offered by specialised travel agencies, such as the Silk Road Railway and the Silk Road Treasure Tours.

Fedorenko, Vladimir; The New
NDRC; Vision
Silk Road Railway

3.51 Trade

The term trade appears thirty-seven times in the *Vision*. Besides the exchange of goods and services, the envisaged development of trade is supposed to boost also foreign investments, the establishment of free trade zones, financial integration, tourism, cultural exchange and international collaboration. Trade is referenced in several other initiatives. For example, Vladimir Fedorenko points to Turkish Minister of Trade Hayati Yazıcı's Silk Road project, which was strongly furthered by the International Forum on the Role of Customs Administration in Promoting and Facilitating Trade among Silk Road Countries, held in Antalya in 2008. Another important trade-related meeting – The International Silk Road Congress: *Rethinking the Road of Trade, Cooperation and Peace* – took place in Istanbul in 2013. As the title formulation suggests, trade is instrumental not only to cooperation but to peace as well. Trade is also a key factor in Russia's project of the Eurasian Economic Union and is bound up with the development of the communications infrastructure. The idea has been often discussed by Vladimir Putin.

Fedorenko, Vladimir; The New
INOMISC; International
NDRC; Vision
Putin, Władymir; U.N.
Yazıcı, Hayati; Turkey

3.52 Transport

Transport is one of the top priorities embraced in several concepts of the New Silk Road. Turkey insists on the simplification of border-crossing procedures concerning transport. The Caucasus countries focus on railway and maritime goods shipments. The American framework has a gas-transporting pipeline at its core. The Chinese New Silk Road project is the most comprehensive of them all. Its various aims and priorities include also transport in two senses. First, the project envisages the construction of land corridors linking China to various Eurasian regions. Second, it foregrounds the development of maritime transport connecting China to South-East Asia and the rest of the world.

Fedorenko, Vladimir; The New
HKTDC; What
Yazıcı, Hayati; Turkey

3.53 Trust

The Asian Development Bank writes about "the spirit of trust and confidence that has evolved through the years among good neighbors and good partners." In his speech in Jakarta in 2013, Jinping Xi described the scope of operations envisaged within the New Road project and prioritised "build[ing] trust and develop[ing] good-neighborliness. Trust is the very foundation of both interpersonal and state-to-state relations." The *Vision* emphasises fostering trust among people, countries and civilisations, with the project defined as "a road towards peace and friendship by enhancing mutual understanding and trust."

Asian Development Bank; The New
NDRC; Vision

3.54 Understanding

"Understanding" is proclaimed to be one of the majora aims of India's Mausam Project, which is supposed to enhance "the understanding of cultural values and concerns" of the Indian Ocean countries. Among its various objectives, the *Vision* lists also mutual understanding among people, organisations, countries and, even, civilisations. In his speech in Jakarta in 2013, Jinping Xi addressed also "enhance[ing] mutual understanding."

NDRC; Vision
The Hans India; What
Xi, Jinping; Speech by Chinese

4. The Silk New World

Nake Kamrany observes that "a new international economic and political order is being born" alongside the New Silk Road. Sebastien Peyrouse writes about "the New World Order," Pepe Escobar about a "New (Silk) World Order," and Peimin Ni about a "New Silk Road World Order." Marcin Kaczmarski discusses "silk globalisation," and Afshin Molavi states that "the 'New Silk Road' is fundamentally transforming our world." Conferences devoted to the theme are held internationally. One of them addressing *The Silk Road, the New World Order* took place in Brussels on 6 October, 2015. Some observers, such as Katarzyna and Mieczysław Sprendel, ask whether China will become a global superpower of the 21st century and, even, replace the US in this role. Many commentators, such as Alice Ekman, notice "new models of international cooperation and global governance." In their Introduction to *Greater China in an Era of Globalization*, Sujian Guo and Baogang Guo quote Oded Shenkar, who writes that the development of China "will change the global landscape" and adds that the process is accompanied by the decreasing relevance of the US as a global economic, political and military power of the previous century. In his review of *Greater China*, Wright Doyle observes that the book discusses two consensuses distinguished by Joshua Cooper Ramo: the "Washington consensus" and the "Beijing consensus." The former, which we have now, touts free market capitalism, free trade, democracy and universal human rights. The latter, proposed by China, endorses sovereignty of states and non-interference in their domestic politics. Helga Zepp-LaRouche states even that the two consensuses and two orders based on them coexist: "There are now two economic and financial systems built on completely different principles. One, the trans-Atlantic system, as an imperial structure, seeks constantly to extend the boundaries of its sphere of power through supranational structures which threaten the sovereignty of other nations." The other is "a new model of cooperation among the nations of the world. (…) they must nonetheless respect the different levels of development, history, culture, and social systems, and above all, respect national sovereignty." Jurij Tawrowski emphasises that the new order is "horizontal rather than vertical," which means that it is not about changing world leadership by having one country replace another in the leader role. Peimin Ni explains that the new horizontal order is multilateral and, as such, is shaped by several countries which "stay away from terms like 'leadership' and 'alliance' instead they prefer words like 'dialogue,' 'partnership,' and 'cooperation.'" Clearly, the descriptions of the New Order are somewhat paradoxical. Some scholars, Peimin Ni among them, underscore its multilateral, multipolar and pluralist character and insist that several countries and their relations are central to it. At the same time, however, many scholars, Peimin Ni among them as well, notice that China performs a very special role and has a very special position in it. When Peimin Ni analyses the philosophical foundations of "the 'Silk Road World Order,' or simply the 'Silk World Order,'" he focuses on two expressions repeatedly used by President of the PRC Jinping Xi: "*mingyun gongtongti* 命运共同体 — community of shared destiny" and "*hezuogongyin* 合作共赢 — cooperation and co-prosperity." He also stresses that such thinking is "deeply rooted in the traditional Chinese culture" and highlights two factors stemming from the Confucian legacy. One of them is the notion of *tianxia* (天下) comprehended as a community of destiny of all under the heaven: "'tianxia' represents an underlying philosophy totally different from the philosophy behind the notion of nation-state. Tianxia entails a sense of seeing all under the heaven as interconnected." The other factor is "*datong* (大同), or Grand Harmony." A similar account is offered by Wenshan Jia, who discerns the rise of a new model of "Confucian global leadership" founded on the five Confucian virtues: *ren* (benevolence), *yi* (righteousness), *li* (propriety), *zhi* (wisdom) and *xin* (integrity). Changping Fang depicts the new order pithily as a "harmonious world." Such an image of the emergent world order is paradoxical in that the pluralistic, multipolar, multilateral and multicultural world is, at the same time, envisaged as the Confucian Great Harmony consistent with traditional Chinese culture.

Jurij Kulincew writes that the New Road "is not China's solo, but a symphony performed by all the interested countries." Mahdi Nazemroaya observes that the New Road entails "a new multi-polar world order": "The New Silk Road and the Eurasian Economic Union not only interface with one another, but they converge and have a symbiotic relationship. They complement one another, but they are more than about Europe,

Asia, or Eurasia. They are about a Silk World that includes every corner of the planet." Yet, the New Road includes, after all, not only Russia's and China's concepts and enterprises, but also initiatives and operations planned and/or launched by other countries. The latter may differ from each other in goals, ways of achieving them and priority areas. As a result, there are multiple New Silk Roads, and, as explained by Ulrich Beck, the major acting agents and founders of these roads are not only states but also private companies and international organisations. Hillary Clinton's initiative, i.e. the American Silk Road, revolves around the concept of helping Afghanistan recover from war damage through developing its contacts with the neighbour countries. Put forward by Ashraf Ghani, the Afghan concept of the Lapis-Lazuli Road (or Azure Route) has different concerns and aims to connect Afghanistan to Europe. Hayati Yazıcı's Turkish Road involves Turkey, the Caucasus countries and Central Asian countries and means simplification and streamlining of border-crossing procedures to facilitate transport. The Great Road as envisaged by Eduard Shevardnadze initially involved pipelines, and later railway transport, but its permanent goal was to make post-Soviet Georgia independent of Russia and turn it into a power in the Caucasus region. India's Mausam Project put forward by Shri Ravindra Singh is about the construction of a maritime communications network across the Indian Ocean, with India as its central node. Naturally, the underlying idea is to enhance India's role and relevance in the region. The Chinese and Russian projects also differ. Russia views the Eurasian Economic Union and Central Asia as instrumental in regaining the superpower status the country enjoyed in the USSR period. In turn, China's priorities include securing natural resources, increasing exports and obtaining infrastructure contracts for Chinese companies.

Also, private companies develop and implement ideas of Roads, big and small. The Islamic Development Bank and its activities designed to boost the development of Muslim communities comply with the Sharia principles. The New Silk Road Company aims to make Dubai a global financial centre. The Singapore-based New Silk Road Investment seeks to expand high-return investments. Germany's DB Schenker, Hong Kong's Silk Route Rail and Poland's Hatrans offer freight rail connections between China and Europe. The Chinese company New Silk Road Group produces and exports silk textiles. The Silk Road Railway of Australia, the Golden

Eagle Luxury Trains of the UK and the Silk Road Treasure Tours of the US advertise railway tourist trips. There are also various other organisations, institutions, private people, concepts, initiatives and enterprises. The Asian Development Bank implements its own programme for the development of "the world's poorest regions." The British Library collaborates with libraries worldwide within the International Dunhuang Project aimed to collect and show to the public exhibits related to the Silk Road. Kyong Park of the US runs a research project investigating New Silk Roads, which focuses on the transformations the cities between Istanbul and Tokyo undergo. The US-based Silk Road Foundation supports research and studies on the Silk Road. The South Korean Silk Road Foundation promotes friendly relations and cooperation between Korea and the Silk Road countries while the Silk Road Reporters of the US publishes information and analyses concerning Central Asia. UNESCO has its own Silk Road-focused programme, including field research, archives, symposia, exhibitions and publications. Its aim is "to promote mutual understanding, tolerance, reconciliation and peace through dialogue." Helga Zepp-LaRouche, who heads the Schiller Institute, has advocated the World Land-Bridge on many occasions since the 1990s. The project focuses on the development of communications infrastructure for peace and prosperity of humanity.

If Jurij Kulincew observes that the New Road is not just "China's solo, but a symphony" performed by various countries, we should add that the musicians have their own different score each. Additionally, the ensemble includes not only various countries, but also companies, organisations and, even, individuals who pursue their private ideas. How the tune sounds depends, therefore, on all the players involved, though not necessarily proportionately or identically. Some instruments are more while other ones less important. Among the countries, companies and organisations involved in the New Road, some are powerful and others are small and less capable. A loud instrument can drown ones that produce delicate sounds, but the latter can also interfere with the melody of the former. In the New Road, the initiatives of big players can develop into greatness owing to the participation of smaller ones. Besides, like in a music ensemble, all the New Road players need others' involvement to accomplish their own aims, and adjusting one's own aims, projects and operations to others' aims, projects and operations is often an important success-determining factor. Even the representatives of China's state-owned Silk Road Fund, with the capital of $40 billion, emphasise that their investments depend on the contribution of private companies. The Asian Infrastructure Investment Bank is becoming an important global bank because fifty-six countries are its members besides China.

The New Road and the Silk New World Order it produces are best understood as an interaction among various initiatives of countries, companies, organisations and individuals. The initiatives are sometimes convergent and sometimes divergent, if not outright conflicting, as companies or states tend to be when they try to win a privileged position in the same area or region. Some initiatives are closely interconnected while other ones are more or less autonomous. All of them, however, or rather interactions among them, contribute to the shape of the New Road and its related Silk New World Order. The New Road is all the time predicated on this interaction, and in this sense, it is legitimate to think of the New Road and the New Order as multilateral, multipolar and pluralistic. If we recall that a similar pluralistic and multicultural world is championed in the Chinese Project, we face anew the paradox inherent in both the New Road and its related new global "silk" order. The pluralistic New Road (with its New Order) would be interconnected with the Great Reborn China advocating for a multicultural world, and the two would mutually fuel each other's development.

In *The Post-American World*, Fareed Zakaria describes a multipolar and hybrid international system as more dynamic, more open and based on mutual connections. Zakaria adds that this system can accommodate the importance of the US, China, India, Russia, Muslim and other countries, but first of all attaches great weight to interactions, agreements and cooperations. What role will China play in this post-American world? Ilya Prigogine explains that the future is unpredictable because it depends on events which have not come to pass yet. However, talking about the New Road, or New Roads, one cannot possibly avoid questions about the future. Much depends on the developments within China and on China's relations with the world. Some inquire about China's position vis-à-vis the US, and others about the viability of China exporting its ideas, values and principles. When Yinhong Shi ponders how China should behave towards the US in the future, he points to the politics of balance dating back to Xiaoping Deng and based on the injunction "to keep old friends and win new ones." Will it hold for the future as well? Of course, this will also depend on the US domestic situation and foreign politics. As far as exporting Chinese ideas is concerned, the topic is vigorously debated in China. Some Chinese intellectuals and politicians have followed Zemin Jiang and underscored the relevance of "soft power" since the 15th Congress of the CPC in 1998. "Soft power," i.e. values, norms and other cultural expressions, is deemed crucial to the country's international image and its global positions and possibilities. Yinhong Shi argues that China must be attractive to the world and its values to be able to inspire others. Some believe, like Changping Fang does, that "in order to achieve its soft-power objectives, China should push for international acceptance of its development model." Others subscribe to a different notion espoused by Bonnie Glaser and Melissa Murphy: "China has never been expansionist and has not pushed a development model on others. This is a very important point. China will never try to export a development model." The outcome of these discussions will essentially affect the Silk Road, the Silk World Order and China as such.

And how is the Silk New World Order related to the past? Giovanni Arrighi builds on Fernand Braudel to develop the concept of successive cycles of the capitalist system, in which the central role was played, chronologically, by Venice, Spain, the Netherlands, the UK and the US. Although the centre of the system continued to shift, the system itself was consistently monocentric. In 2002, Arrighi noticed indications of a new centre of capital accumulation emerging in East Asia. Can the CPC-ruled country become another centre of the global capitalist system? Janet Abu-Lughod describes the world from "before European hegemony" and calls it "the thirteenth-century world system," though, importantly, she means the Old World of three continents: Africa, Europe and Asia. Abu-Lughod emphasises the multicentricity of that 13th-century order of the Old World, which consisted of eight interconnected regions; West Europe, the East Mediterranean, the Red Sea, the Arab Sea, the Persian Gulf, the Bengal Gulf, the China Seas and Central Asia. She highlights the crucial role the Indian Ocean played in this system as a communication channel. Oceaning navigation and shipping connected remote coasts, and ports were sites where maritime routes intersected with land roads spreading towards distant regions of Africa, Europe and Asia. The Indian Ocean was divided into three major zones under the influence of superpowers of the day. The western zone encompassed the

Arab Sea and was Arab-dominated. The middle part was India's zone. The eastern coast of the Indian Ocean together with the China Seas was controlled by China. Abu-Lughod emphasises, however, that the system was polycentric, and no centre, or no superpower, controlled the whole.

Are we facing the decline of the world capitalist system built by Europeans, which allows only once centre while the emergent Silk New World Order is polycentric, just like the thirteenth-century system? Will the Indian Ocean be central also the new order? Kirti Chaudhuri describes the key global role of the Indian Ocean from the birth of Islam to the rise of European colonial powers. In turn, Andre Gunder Frank highlights the important role the Atlantic Ocean played in the efforts of European colonial powers to build a new global capitalist system, which added New Worlds to the Old World. However, in 1991, Abu-Lughod notices "a displacement of the center of a global system from the Atlantic to the Pacific Ocean." Arrighi explains: "In 1980, trans-Pacific trade began to surpass trans-Atlantic trade in value." So what role do oceans play in the Silk New World Order? Will the role of the communications centre still belong to the Pacific, or will it be taken over by the Indian Ocean? Or, perhaps, the central communications role will now belong to the land New Silk Road, which connects distant regions and cities of Eurasia and Africa to each other?

Abu-Lughod, Janet; Before
Arrighi, Giovanni; The Long
Beck, Ulrich; Władza
Chaudhuri, Kirti; Trade
Cooper Ramo, Joshua; The Beijing
Doyle, Wright; Greater
Escobar, Pepe; U.S.
Fang, Changping; Comparison; qtd. in Glaser, Bonnie S.; Melissa E. Murphy; Soft
Frank, Andre Gunder; Reorient
Guo, Sujian; Baogang Guo; Introduction
IES; The Silk
Jia, Wenshan; Chiglobalization
Kaczmarski, Marcin; Jedwabna
Nazemroaya, Mahdi Darius; Neither
Nazemroaya, Mahdi Darius; The Silk
Ni, Peimin, The underlying
Peyrouse, Sebastien; Building
Prigogine, Ilya; Isabelle Stengers; Z chaosu
Shenkar, Oded; The Chinese

Shi, Yinhong; The Roles
The Hans India; What
Yazıcı, Hayati; Turkey
Zepp-LaRouche, Helga; The New Silk Road Leads
Zakaria, Fareed; Post
Тавровский, Юрий; Новые

References[8]

A crucial feature of the China's crude oil maritime routes, in: South Front, 24.08.2015. https://southfront.org/china-crude-oil-maritime-routes/

Abu-Lughod, Janet. *Before European hegemony: The world system A.D. 1250–1350.* New York 1991.

Acar, A. Zafer, Bentyn, Zbigniew & Kocaoğlu, Batuhan. Logistic performance development of the countries on the path along the new silk road. in: Research Gate, https://www.researchgate.net/publication/292059588_Logistic_performance_development_of_the_countries_on_the_path_along_the_new_silk_road

Advantour. http://www.advantour.com/uzbekistan/trains.htm

Albert, Eleanor. The Shanghai Cooperation Organization, in: Council on Foreign Relations, 14.10.2015, http://www.cfr.org/china/shanghai-cooperation-organization/p10883.

Alderman, Liz. Port w Pireusie rozkwita po przejęciu przez Chińczyków, in: Vox Europe, 16.10.2012. http://www.voxeurop.eu/pl/content/article/2881051-port-w-pireusie-rozkwita-po-przejeciu-przez-chinczykow

Alexander, Harriet. World's longest train journey ends in Madrid, in: The Telegraph, 22.06.2014, http://www.telegraph.co.uk/news/worldnews/europe/spain/11284911/Worlds-longest-train-journey-ends-in-Madrid.html

Almaty Agreement. whc.unesco.org/document/139778, 25.11.2015.

Andrea, Alfred J. & Levi, Scott C. The Silk Roads: Afro-Eurasian connectivity across the ages, in: George Modelski & Robert A. Denmnark (Eds.), *World System History*, vol. I, London 2009.

Aneja, Atul. Zhengzhou emerges a major hub along the New Silk Road, in: The Hindu, 22.12.2015. http://www.thehindu.com/news/international/zhengzhou-emerges-a-major-hub-along-the-new-silk-road/article8018810.ece

Aneja, Atul. China developing soft-power infra along Silk Road, in: The Hindu, 8.05.2016. http://www.thehindu.com/news/international/china-developing-softpower-infra-along-silk-road/article8572831.ece

---

8 In entries referring to websites, the date of access is 11 August 2016, unless another date is indicated.

Arrighi, Giovanni. *The long twentieth century: Money, power, and the origins of our times*. London 2002.

Arts & Humanities Research Council. The Silk Road: Contextualising a cultural journey through time. http://www.ahrc.ac.uk/research/casestud ies/thesilkroad/

Asante, Molefi Kete. *The history of Africa: The quest for eternal harmony*. New York 2014.

Asia Landmark Fund LTD. http://whalewisdom.com/filer/asia-landmark-fund-ltd

Asian Development Bank. http://www.adb.org/

Asian Development Bank. *The New Silk Road: Ten years of the Central Asia Regional Economic Cooperation Program*. Mandaluyong 2011.

Asian Infractructure Investment Bank. http://www.aiib.org/

Asian Infrastructure Investment Bank. Introduction. http://euweb.aiib.org/ html/aboutus/introduction/aiib/?show=0

Atlanta Travel. New route of Afrosiab high speed train Tashkent – Karshi, http://openuzbekistan.com/news/tashkent_karshi

Azaaroll, Augusto. *An early history of horsemanship*. Leiden 1985.

Azerbaijan. History. http://www.azerbaijans.com/content_829_en.html

Azerbaijan State News Agency. Eduard Shevardnadze: President of Azerbaijan Heydar Aliyev has great services in creating and developing of "Great Silk Way" Project. 17.09.2003. http://azertag.az/en/print/546677

Aziz, Zeti Akhtar. Potential role of Islamic finance in strengthening the The New Silk Road. 28.03.2007. https://www.bis.org/review/r070330f.pdf

BAA Global Conference. https://globalconference.bocconialumni.it/en/pro gram/index.html

Babayeva, Fatma. Azerbaijan, Georgia, Kazakhstan create railway consortium, in: Azernews, 14.04.2016. http://www.azernews.az/business/95155.html

Banerjee, Dipankar. China's One Belt One Road Initiative – An Indian perspective, in: *Perspective. ISEAS*, no 14, 2016.

Bazo, Mariana. China and Peru agree to study transcontinental rail link, in: *Reuters*, 22.05.2015. http://www.reuters.com/article/us-china-latam-railway-idUSKBN0O802P20150523

BBC News. US-made Tajik-Afghan bridge opens, 26.08.2007. http://news.bbc.co.uk/2/hi/asia-pacific/6964429.stm

BBC News. Nicaragua Congress approves ocean-to-ocean canal plan, 13.06.2013. http://www.bbc.com/news/world-latin-america-22899744

BBC News. China to build new East Africa railway line, 12.05.2014. http://www.bbc.com/news/world-africa-27368877

BBC News. Is China-Pakistan 'silk road' a game-changer? 22.04.2015. http://www.bbc.com/news/world-asia-32400091

BCIM Car Rally 2013. https://www.google.com/maps/d/viewer?mid=1SJU Do8ZVNDZhpiDARJBFOMz5ORk&hl=en_US

Beck, Ulrich. *Power in the global age: A new global political economy*. Cambridge, UK, and Malden, MA 2005.

Beijing Capital International Airport Co. Ltd. http://en.bcia.com.cn/

Belgrade Meeting. Belgrade 2014. http://www.china-ceec-summit.gov.rs/doc/CHINA%20SEE%20SUMMIT%20Belgrade%20Meeting%20bro chure%202014.pdf

Belt and Road Summit. http://www.beltandroadsummit.hk/en/informa tion_centre/about_bars.html

Billington, Michael. Xi Jinping's New Silk Road: Reviving Confucian Culture, in: *EIR*, 10.04.2015. http://www.larouchepub.com/other/2015/4215xi_confucian_culture.html

Bińczyk, Beata. Inauguracja pociągu relacji Łódź-Xiamen (Chiny), in: *Izba Celna w Łodzi*. 31.08.2015. http://www.lodz.scelna.gov.pl/wiadomosci/aktualnosci/-/asset_publisher/vET0/content/inauguracja-pociagu-relacji-lodz-xiamen-China;jsessionid=29DC8C7D28377B1730D6FFF596305 490?redirect=http%3A%2F%2Fwww.lodz.scelna.gov.pl%2Fstart%3Bjsessionid%3D29DC8C7D28377B1730D6FFF596305490%3Fp_p_id%3D101_INSTANCE_he8D%26p_p_lifecycle%3D0%26p_p_state%3Dnormal%26p_p_mode%3Dview%26p_p_col_id%3Dcolumn-1%26p_p_col_count%3D2

Bipul, Chatterjee & Surendar, Singh. An Opportunity for India in Central Asia, in: *The Diplomat*, 04.05.2015. http://thediplomat.com/2015/05/an-opportunity-for-india-in-central-asia/

Bland, Daniel. China to back US$10bn Brazil-Peru railway project, in: BNAmericas, 13.05.2015. http://www.bnamericas.com/en/news/infra structure/china-to-back-us10bn-brazil-peru-railway-project1

Blinova, Ekaterina. Gold Yuan. Post-Dollar World Order Emerging in Eurasia, in: Sputnik International, 15.09.2016. https://sputniknews.com/politics/201609151045341538-gold-yuan-china-dollar-eurasia/. Accessed on 15 December 2016.

Bondaz, Antoine. Rebalancing China's geopolitics, in: *China Analysis*, June 2015.

Bradsher, Keith. Hauling new treasure along the Silk Road, in: The New York Times, 20.07.2013. http://www.nytimes.com/2013/07/21/business/global/hauling-new-treasure-along-the-silk-road.html?pagewanted=all&_r=0

Brugier, Camille. China's way: the New Silk Road, in: *BRIEF. European Union Institute for Security Studies*, no 14, 2014.

Brzeziński, Zbigniew. A Geostrategy for Eurasia, in: *Foreign Affairs*, September/October 1997. https://www.foreignaffairs.com/articles/asia/1997-09-01/geostrategy-eurasia

Burgen, Stephen. The Silk Railway: Freight train from China pulls up in Madrid, in: The Guardian, 10.12.2014. https://www.theguardian.com/business/2014/dec/10/silk-railway-freight-train-from-china-pulls-into-madrid

Caravanistan. Irkeshtam Pass: Osh-Kashgar. http://caravanistan.com/border-crossings/kyrgyzstan/irkeshtam-pass/

Caravanistan. Torugart Pass. http://caravanistan.com/border-crossings/kyrgyzstan/torugart-pass/

Caron, Pierre. China gets French wine in exchange for chemicals on first run by 'New Silk Road' train, in: Vice News, 21.04.2016. https://news.vice.com/article/china-gets-french-wine-in-exchange-for-chemicals-on-first-run-by-new-silk-road-train

CASA 1000. http://www.casa-1000.org/

Casey, Michel. Investors needed for Kyrgyz Hydropower Projects, in: *The Diplomat*, 20.01.2016. http://thediplomat.com/2016/01/investors-needed-for-kyrgyz-hydropower-projects/

CC.TV. Silk Road International Arts Festival opens in X'an, 09.16.2015. http://english.cntv.cn/2015/09/16/VIDE1442400121762292.shtml. Accessed on 17 June 2017.

Centre for Transport Strategies. New Silk Road's test train returns to Ukraine. 22.04.2016. http://en.cfts.org.ua/news/new_silk_roads_test_train_returns_to_ukraine

Chan, Vinicy. Silk Road Fund Said to Mull Bid for $2 Billion Glencore Mine. Bloomberg, 6.07.2016. https://www.bloomberg.com/news/arti cles/2016-07-06/silk-road-fund-said-to-weigh-offer-for-2-billion-glen core-mine. Accessed on 12 January 2017.

Chaudhuri, Kirti. *Trade and civilisation in the Indian Ocean: An economic history from the rise of Islam to 1750*. Cambridge 1985.

Chen, Xiangming & Mardemusz, Julia. China and Europe: Reconnecting across a New Silk Road, in: *The European Financial Review*, 10.02.2015. http://www.europeanfinancialreview.com/?p=4143

Cheng, Irene. The New Silk Road, in: *Russia/China 1920/2004*, pp. 30–31. New York 2004.

Cheng, Shuaihua. China's new Silk Road: Implications for the US, in: *ICTSD*, 1.06.2015. http://www.ictsd.org/opinion/china

Cheng, Yugang. Build China's soft power within the Context of Globalization, in: *Guoji Guangcha*, February 2007.

Chernov, Vitaly. Russia's interests beyond 'silk' projects, in: *Port News*, 25.06.2015. http://portnews.ru/comments/print/1981/?backurl=/comments/

China. Xi'an. http://hua.umf.maine.edu/China/xian.html

China Copyright and Media. Outline of the National 11th Five Year Plan Period Cultural Development Plan, 13.09.2006. https://chinacopyright andmedia.wordpress.com/2006/09/13/outline-of-the-national-11th-five-year-plan-period-cultural-development-plan/

China COSCO Holdings Company Limited. http://en.chinacosco.com/

China Daily. Opening ceremony of 1st Silk Road International Arts Festival held in Xi'an, 14.09.2014. http://www.chinadaily.com.cn/culture/2014-09/14/content_18595072.htm

China Daily. Silk Road Cultural Journey launched in NW China, 21.09.2014. http://www.chinadaily.com.cn/culture/2014-09/21/content_18635089_2.htm

China Daily. Xinjiang eyes tourist boom with new airport, 02.08.2015. http://www.chinadaily.com.cn/china/60thxjannivesary/2015-08/02/con tent_21476711.htm

China Daily. Chinese fund eyes Glencore's gold mine in Kazakhstan, 08.07.2016. http://www.china.org.cn/business/2016-07/08/content_38835273.htm

China Daily. CPC communicates with the word for global economic governance. http://www.chinadaily.com.cn/china/2016-10/15/content_27071617. htm. Accessed on 15 October 2016.

China Discovery. 8 Days Silk Road Tour with Chengdu Panda. http://www. chinadiscovery.com/china-tours-from-chengdu/silk-road-chengdu-pan da.html

China Heritage Newsletter. China Maritime Silk Road Museum. no 1, March, 2005. http://www.chinaheritagequarterly.org/articles.php?searchterm=001_ maritimesilk.inc&issue=001

China Highlights. Maritime Silk Road. http://www.chinahighlights.com/ travelguide/maritime-silk-road.htm

China Investments Research. Chinese overseas lending dominated by One Belt One Road strategy. http://www.chinainvestmentresearch.org/press/ chinese-overseas-lending-dominated-by-one-belt-one-road-strategy/

China Knowlegde. The Shiji 史記 "Records of the [Grand] Scribe". http:// www.chinaknowledge.de/Literature/Historiography/shiji.html

China Nonferrous Metal Mining. http://www.cnmc.com.cn/outlineen. jsp?column_no=1202

China Ocean Shipping Company. http://en.cosco.com/col/col764/index. html

China Overseas Holdings Limited. https://www.cohl.com/en/Page/list/94. html

China Overseas Ports Holding Company Pakistan (Pvt.) Ltd. http://coph cgwadar.com.192-185-11-8.secure19.win.hostgator.com/

Chinese Government, China Council for International Cooperation on Environment and Development. Important Speech of Xi Jinping at Peripheral Diplomacy Work Conference. 30.10.2013. http://www.cciced. net/encciced/newscenter/latestnews/201310/t20131030_262608.html

Chinese Turkestan. in: Encyclopaedia Iranica. http://www.iranicaonline. org/articles/chinese-turkestan-ii

Clinton, Hillary Rodham. Remarks on India and the United States: A vision for the 21st Century. http://www.state.gov/secretary/20092013clinton/ rm/2011/07/168840.htm

Clover, Charles & Hornby, Lucy. China's great game: Road to a new empire, in: The Big Read. Financial Times, http://www.ft.com/intl/cms/s/2/6e098274-587a-11e5-a28b-50226830d644.html#axzz49UHBILYi

CNTO, Silk Road. in: China like never before. http://www.cnto.org/journeys/silk-road/

Coase, Ronald. The market for goods and the market for ideas, in: *The American Economic Review*, vol. 64, no 2, 1974.

Coburn, Leonard L. Central Asia: Pipelines Are the New Silk Road. https://www.iaee.org/en/publications/newsletterdl.aspx?id=113. *Accessed on 12 January 2017.*

Cohen, David. China's 'second opening': Grand ambitions but a long road ahead, in: *China Analysis*, Jume 2005.

Cole, Juan. The Chinese are coming: First 'New Silk Road' train reaches Iran's capital, in: *Informed Commend*, 17.02.2016, http://www.juancole.com/2016/02/the-chinese-are-coming-first-new-silk-road-train-reaches-irans-capital.html

Consortium Chemico. http://www.chemico-group.com/index.php?option=com_content&view=article&id=566&Itemid=136, http://www.silkroadfund.com.cn/enwap/27363/index.html

Cooper Ramo, Joshua. *The Beijing Consensus: Notes on the physics of Chinese nature.* London 2004.

Cooperation between China and Central and Eastern European Country. 22.06.2016. http://www.china-ceec.org/eng/

Covington, Richard. Hearts of the New Silk Roads, in: *Aramco World*, vol. 59, no 1, 2008. http://archive.aramcoworld.com/issue/200801/hearts.of.the.new.silk.roads.htm

Daily News. Marmaray tunnel paves way for 'Iron Silk Road'. 29.10.2013. http://www.hurriyetdailynews.com/marmaray-tunnel-paves-way-for-iron-silk-road.aspx?pageID=238&nID=56995&NewsCatID=345

Daly, John C.K. China and Kazakhstan to construct a Trans-Kazakhstan Railway Line From Khorgos to Aktau, in: *Global Research and Analysis*, 20.05.2015. http://www.jamestown.org/programs/edm/single/?tx_ttnews%5Btt_news%5D=43934&cHash=30f9f55ee09e00fc849b8d0e8572761b#.V7XHlxK1B0Q

Davis, Jonathan. Trio sign up for Turkmen gas, in: upstream, 25.04.2008. http://www.upstreamonline.com/live/article1156011.ece

DB Schenker. https://www.dbschenker.com/global/about/profile

DB Schenker. DB Schenker starts first freight train from Hamburg to Zhengzou. http://www.logistics.dbschenker.at/log-at-en/news-media/news/8198260/20140903-china-hamburg-train.html

Dehghan, Saeed Kamali. China's Silk Road revival steams ahead as cargo train arrives in Iran, in: The Guardian, 15.02.2016. https://www.theguardian.com/business/2016/feb/15/chinas-silk-road-revival-steams-ahead-as-cargo-train-arrives-in-iran.

Devirupa, Mitra. With Chabahar text finalised, India's dream of a road to Afghanistan gathers speed, in: *The Wire*, 13.04.2016. http://thewire.in/29174/with-chabahar-text-finalised-indias-dream-of-a-road-to-afghanistan-gathers-speed/

Diálogo Chino. The Transcontinental Railroad. http://dialogochino.net/the-twin-ocean-railroad/

Dollar, David. China's rise as a regional and global power: The AIIB and the 'one belt, one road', in: *Brookings*, Summer 2015. http://www.brookings.edu/research/papers/2015/07/china-regional-global-power-dollar

Doyle, G. Wright. Greater China in an era of globalization. Review, in: *Chinese Society & Politics*, 20.11.2012. http://www.globalchinacenter.org/analysis/chinese-society-politics/

Dubai Airports. http://www.dubaiairports.ae/

Dubai International Financial Centre. https://www.difc.ae/public-register/new-silk-road-company-ltd

Dubé, François. China's experiment in Djibouti, in: *The Diplomat*, 5.10.2016. http://thediplomat.com/2016/10/chinas-experiment-in-djibouti/. Accessed on 6 January 2016.

Dudała, Jerzy. Wielki potencjał wpółpracy na linii Europa-Chiny, in: *wnp.pl*, 23.04.2015. http://logistyka.wnp.pl/wielki-potencjal-wspolpracy-na-linii-europa-China,248928_1_0_0.html

Dworakowska, Katarzyna. Port morski Hong Kong, in: *Seaoo*, 12.08.2015. https://www.seaoo.com/blog/port-morski-hong-kong/

Dyussembekova, Zhazira. Silk Road renewed with launch of new commercial transit route, in: *The Astana Times*, 21.01.2016. http://astanatimes.com/2016/01/silk-road-renewed-with-launch-of-new-commercial-transit-route/

dziennik.pl. Uzbecka kolej lepsza od polskiej, 30.08.2011. http://wiadomosci. dziennik.pl/swiat/artykuly/353477,uzbecka-kolej-lepsza-od-polskiej.html

East Time. Uzbekistan to launch A High-Speed Train "Tashkent – Bukhara", 20.04.2016. http://easttime.info/news/uzbekistan/uzbekistan-launch-high-speed-train-tashkent-bukhara

Ekman, Alice. China: Reshaping the global order?, in: *Alert. ISS EU*, no 29, 24.07.2015. http://www.iss.europa.eu/publications/detail/article/china-reshaping-the-global-order/

Encyclopaedia Iranica. Chinese Turkestan in pre-Islamic times. http://www. iranicaonline.org/articles/chinese-turkestan-ii

Engdahl, F. William. China's New Roads to Russia, in: *New Eastern Outlook*, 28.05.2015. http://journal-neo.org/2015/05/28/china-s-new-roads-to-russia/

Engdahl, F. William. China Quietly Prepares Golden Alternative to Dollar System; in: *NEO. New Eastern Outlook*, 18.05.2016. http://journal-neo.org/2016/05/18/china-quietly-prepares-golden-alternative-to-dollar-system/. Accessed on 15 January 2016.

Escobar, Pepe. U.S. Wakes up to "New (Silk) World Order", in: *Asia Times*, 15.05.2015. http://atimes.com/2015/05/u-s-wakes-up-to-new-silk-world-order/

Eurasian Business Briefing. New Silk Road transport route opens between Harbin and Ekaterinburg, 05.03.2016. http://www.eurasianbusiness briefing.com/new-silk-road-transport-route-opens-harbin-ekatrinburg/

Eurasian Economic Union. http://www.eaeunion.org/?lang=en#info

EuroBelarus. As the binational industrial park near Minsk enters a new development stage, problems remain, 30.12.2015. http://en.eurobelarus. info/news/economy/2015/12/30/as-the-binational-industrial-park-near-minsk-enters-a-new.html

Fallon, Theresa. The New Silk Road: Xi Jinping's grand strategy for Eurasia, in: *American Foreign Policy Interests*, no 37, 2015.

Fang, Changping. Comparison of Chinese and U.S. soft power and its implications for China, in: *Shijie Jingji Yu Zhengzhi*, 1.07.2007.

Fedorenko, Vladimir. The New Silk Road initiatives in Central Asia, in: *Rethinking Paper*, no 10, August 2013.

Forest, Dave. Prime Meridians: A Journey Along Copper's New Silk Road, Pierce Points, 31.10.2015. http://piercepoints.com/prime-meridians-a-journey-along-coppers-new-silk-road/. Acccessed on 12 January 2017.

Forrest, Brett. The New Silk Road, in: *National Geographic*, July 2016. http://ngm.nationalgeographic.com/2010/08/new-silk-road/forrest-text

Forss, Pearl & Morse, Anthony. China's New Silk Road, in: *Channel News Asia*, 03.10.2015. http://www.channelnewsasia.com/news/asiapacific/in-pictures-china-s-new/2167304.html

Forum Regionalne Polska-Chiny. Tomasz Grzelak. http://www.PolandChina.lodzkie.pl/prelegenci/item/53-tomasz-grzelak/53-tomasz-grzelak

Four Seasons Hotel Dubai International Financial Centre. http://www.fourseasons.com/dubaidifc/

Frank, Andre Gunder. *ReOrient: Global economy in the Asian age*. Berkeley 1998.

Frankwaterloo. New Silk Road started from China to Germany, Ukriane, Turkey, France... https://frankwaterloo.wordpress.com/2016/04/07/new-silk-road-started-from-china-to-germany-ukriane-turkey-france/

Frąk, Michał. Polak na Jedwabnym Szlaku. http://wyborcza.biz/biznes/1,147752,19399385,polak-na-jedwabnym-szlaku-pekin-chce-by-pociagi-do-chin-jezdzily.html?disableRedirects=true

Fremde Impulse. The city wall provides protection for merchants from near and far. https://www.lwl.org/LWL/Kultur/fremde-impulse/die_impulse/Impuls-Duisburg-Handel-Mittelalter/?lang=en

Gasimli, Vusal. The New Baku International Seaport: A nexus for the New Silk Road, in: *Global Research and Analysis*, 02.10.2015. http://www.jamestown.org/single/?tx_ttnews[tt_news]=44442&tx_ttnews[backPid]=7&cHash=2ba96fa4dd2f20e18e98cb681e3c64e6#.V0MHBSFO10Q

Ge, Huang. Xiamen trade fair to focus on development of 'Belt and Road,' in: *Global Times*, 21.08.2015. http://www.globaltimes.cn/content/936817.shtml

Gegeshidze, Archil. The New Silk Road: A Georgian perspective. http://sam.gov.tr/wp-content/uploads/2012/02/Archil Gegeshidze.pdf

Geodis. Eurasia Rail Network. http://www.geodiswilson.com/PageFiles/25727/2015_Geodis_Nordics_Rail_service.pdf

Gilad, Uri, Vicziany, Marika & Zhu, Xuan. At the heart of the Silk Road: the cultural heritage of Kashgar, in: *Antiquity*. http://antiquity.ac.uk/projgall/gilad321/

Glaser, Bonnie S. & Murphy, Melissa E. Soft power with Chinese characteristics, in: *CSIS*, 10.03.2009. https://www.csis.org/analysis/soft-power-chinese-characteristics

Global Forum Baku 2016. http://baku.unaoc.org/session_title/networking-session-the-new-silk-road-a-route-of-peace/

Glosserman, Brad. China's smile diplomacy, in: South China Morning Post, 1.04.2004. http://www.scmp.com/article/450592/chinas-smile-diplomacy

Godement, François. Introduction, in: *China Analysis*, June, 2015. http://www.ecfr.eu/page/-/China_analysis_belt_road.pdf

Golden Eagle Luxury Trains. http://www.goldeneagleluxurytrains.com/

Golden Eagle Luxury Trains. Silk Road. http://www.goldeneagleluxurytrains.com/journeys/silk-road/eastbound/

Gonzales, Iris C. Philippines seen to benefit from China's New Silk Road, in: *The Philippine Star*, 11.01.2016. http://www.philstar.com/business/2016/01/11/1541307/philippines-seen-benefit-chinas-new-silk-road

Goñi, Uki. Argentinian congress approves deal with China on satellite space station, in: The Guardian, 26.02.2015. https://www.theguardian.com/world/2015/feb/26/argentina-congress-china-satellite-space-station. Accessed on 9 September 2016.

Good Hope Logistics. Freight train schedules from Zhengzhou China to Europe. https://www.goodhopefreight.com/info/logistics-knowledge/freight-train-schedules.html

Grand Valley State University. Peimin Ni. https://www.gvsu.edu/philosophy/peimin-ni-22.htm

Grieger, Gisela. Nicaragua: The Chinese inter-ocean canal project, in: *At a glance: European Parliament*, May 2015. http://www.europarl.europa.eu/RegData/etudes/ATAG/2015/556980/EPRS_ATA%282015%29556980_EN.pdf

Gruszczyński, Bartosz. Chińskie miasto w centrum Białorusi – park przemysłowy "Wielki Kamień," in: *Państwo Środka*, 02.03.2016. http://panstwosrodka.pl/2016/03/02/chinskie-miasto-w-centrum-bialorusi-park-przemyslowy-wielki-kamien/

Guo, Sujian & Gou, Baogang. Introduction, in: Sujian Guo & Baogang Guo (Eds.), *Greater China in an Era of Globalization*. Lanham 2010.

Gurt, Marat, Auyezov, Olzhas, Golubkova, Katya & Merriman, Jane. Turkmenistan starts work on gas link to Afghanistan, Pakistan, India, in: *Reuters*, 13.12.2015. http://uk.reuters.com/article/turkmenistan-gas-pipeline-idUKKBN0TW05Q20151213

Guzek, Paweł. Sangtuda -2 ponownie produkuje energię elektryczną. http://tadzykistan.info/prasa-mainmenu-9/1074-sangtuda-2-ponownie-produkuje-energie-elektryczn

Gücüyener, Ayhan. Alyat Port: A key component for the 'Revival of the Silk Road', in: *Hazar Strateji Enstitüsü*, 10.10.2014. http://www.hazar.org/blogdetail/blog/alyat_port_a_key_component_for_the_%E2%80%98revival_of_the_silk_road%E2%80%99_914.aspx

Harold, Frank. Herat, in: *Silk Road Seatle Project*. https://depts.washington.edu/silkroad/cities/afghanistan/herat.html

Hatrans Logistics. http://www.hatrans.pl/

Hatrans Logistics. New Silk Road. Fastest connection China-Europe. http://www.PolandChina.lodzkie.pl/files/3.pdf

Hatrans Logistics. Train China to Lodz. http://www.hatrans.pl/en/rail.html

Hawser, Anita. Financing New Silk Road, in: *Global Finance*, November 2013. http://www.efa-group.net/assets/news/Global_Finance_IslamicTF_Report.pdf

HKTDC. Belt and Road Summit, 18.05.2016, Hong Kong. http://beltandroad.hktdc.com/en/index.aspx

HKTDC. What is Belt and Road Initiative. http://beltandroad.hktdc.com/en/about-the-belt-and-road-initiative/about-the-belt-and-road-initiative.aspx

HKTDT Research. The Belt and Road Initiative, 21.01.2016. http://china-trade-research.hktdc.com/business-news/article/One-Belt-One-Road/The-Belt-and-Road-Initiative/obor/en/1/1X000000/1X0A36B7.htm

Hodge, Adam. Karakoram Highway: China's treacherous Pakistan corridor, in: *The Diplomat*, 30.07.2013. http://thediplomat.com/2013/07/karakoram-highway-chinas-treacherous-pakistani-corridor/

Hogg, Rachael. China conference: New Silk Road gets back on the rails, in: *Automotive Logistics*, 20.04.2016. http://automotivelogistics.media/news/china-conference-new-silk-road-gets-back-on-the-rails

Hołdys, Andrzej. Kanał Nikaraguański, in: *Wiedza i Życie*, 21.11.2013. http://www.wiz.pl/8,1421.html

Hope, Kerin. Greece sells controlling stake in Piraeus port, in: *Financila Times*, 08.04.2016. https://www.ft.com/content/895aac42-fd98-11e5-b5f5-070dca6d0a0d?mhq5j=e2

Hu, Angang. Harmony is also the last word; it has become China's greatest power, in: *Zhongguo Xinwen She*, 12.10.2016.

Hu, Jian. China's responsibilities and the road of peaceful development, in: *Xiandai Guoji Guanxi*, 20.07.2007.

Hu, Jintao. Full text of Hu Jintao's Report to the 17th Party Congress, in: *Xinhua*, 24.10.2008. http://news.xinhuanet.com/english/2007-10/24/content_6938749.htm

Hu Jintao's report at 18th Party Congress, in: *Voltaire Network*, 17.11.2012. http://www.voltairenet.org/article176641.html

Huang, Flora. Yiwu Market survival guide – China, HG.org Legal Sources. http://www.hg.org/article.asp?id=30200

IES. The Silk Road, The New World Order and EU-China Relations. www.ies.be/node/3372

INOMISC. International Silkroad Congress, 30.10.2013. https://inomics.com/international-silkroad-congress-10-actr-conference-istanbul

Institute of Chinese Studies. Bangladesh-India-China-Myanmar Forum. http://www.icsin.org/bangladesh-india-china-myanmar-forum

International Law Office of Dr. Behrooz Akhlaghi & Associates. *Bi-Weekly Newsletter*, no 16. http://www.akhlaghi.net/wp-content/uploads/2015/02/Transit-Transport-Iran-its-Neighbouring-Countries-16th-Bi-Weekly-N-A-November-22-2014.pdf

International North-South Transport Corridor. http://www.instc-org.ir/Pages/Home_Page.aspx

Islamic Development Bank. http://www.isdb-pilot.org/

Islamic Development Bank. Aid for trade case story: Silk Road Project Azerbaijan. https://www.oecd.org/aidfortrade/47720787.pdf

Islamic Development Bank. Silk Road Project Azerbaijan. https://www.oecd.org/aidfortrade/47720787.pdf

Islamic Development Bank Group. Special Program for Central Asia. http://www.isdb-am41.org/wp-content/uploads/2016/05/SPCA-Final-Document.pdf

Istanbul Ataturk Airport. http://www.ataturkairport.com/en-EN/Pages/Main.aspx

JCtransnet. Best freight rate from Shanghai to Hamburg. http://www.jctrans.net/Freightshow/details-2015.html

Jędrzejczak, Agnieszka. Pierwszy pociąg z Łodzi do Xiamen. Nowe połączenie z Chinami, in: *Nasze Miasto*, 27.08.2015. http://lodz.naszemiasto.pl/artykul/pierwszy-pociag-z-lodzi-do-xiamen-nowe-polaczenie-z-chinami,3490884,artgal,t,id,tm.html

Jia, Qingguo. One Belt, One Road: Urgent clarifications and discussions of a few major questions, in: *Renmin Luntan*, 19.03.2015.

Jia, Wenshan. Chiglobalization? A cultural argument, in: Sujian Guo & Baogang Guo (Eds.), *Greater China in an Era of Globalization*. Lanham 2010.

Johnson, Keith. In odyssey for Chinese, Greece sells its fabled Port of Piraeus, in: *Foreign Policy*, 8.04.2016. http://foreignpolicy.com/2016/04/08/in-odyssey-for-chinese-greece-sells-its-fabled-port-of-piraeus/

Jones, William. Zepp-LaRouche presents EIR's New Silk Road Report at Beijing Symposium, in: *New World Land Bridge*, 6.10.2015, https://worldlandbridge.com/2015/10/06/zepp-larouche-presents-eirs-new-silk-road-report-at-beijing-symposium/

Kaczmarski, Marcin. Jedwabna globalizacja. Chińska wizja ładu międzynarodowego, in: *Punkt Widzenia*, no 60. 2016, https://www.osw.waw.pl/sites/default/files/pw_60_pl_jedwabna_globalizacja_net.pdf

Kaczmarski, Marcin. Nowy Jedwabny Szlak: uniwersalne narzędzie chińskiej polityki, in: *Ośrodek Studiów Wschodnich*, http://www.osw.waw.pl/pl/publikacje/komentarze-osw/2015-02-10/nowy-jedwabny-szlak-uniwersalne-narzedzie-chinskiej-polityki

Kakar, Javed Hamim. President Ghani arrives to red-carpet welcome in Baku, in: *Pajhwok Afghan News*, 22.12.2015. http://www.pajhwok.com/en/2015/12/22/president-ghani-arrives-red-carpet-welcome-baku

Kaliński, Adam. Na nowy Jedwabny Szlak Chiny dają na początek 40 mld dol, in: *Obserwator Finansowy*, 27.01.2015. https://www.obserwatorfi nansowy.pl/tematyka/makroekonomia/na-nowy-jedwabny-szlak-China-daja-na-poczatek-40-mld-dol/

Kamalova, Gyuzel & Kuzmina, Tatyana. New transportation opportunities for Trans-Caspian Route: Nomad express container train welcomed in Baku, in: *Tengrinews*, 10.08.2015. https://en.tengrinews.kz/industry_ infrastructure/New-transportation-opportunities-for-Trans-Caspian-Route-261459/

Kamrany, Nake M. China's new world order: Sharing global prosperity through connectivity of the Silk Route countries, in: *The World Post*, 3.06.2015. www.huffingtonpost.com/nake-m-kamrany

Kane, Frank. New Silk Road can smooth Dubai's path to top role in finance, in: The National Business, 18.04.2012. http://www.thenational.ae/busi ness/industry-insights/economics/new-silk-road-can-smooth-dubais-path-to-top-role-in-finance

Kaz Minerals. Aktogay. http://www.kazminerals.com/en/operations/akto gay. Accessed on 6 December 2016.

KazWorldInfo. Trade Zone opens at Alaw Pass. http://kazworld.info/? p=5249. Accessed on 12 October 2016.

Keim, Anna Beth & Kahn, Sulmaan. Can China and Turkey build a new Silk Road? in: *Yale Global*, 18.01.2013. http://yaleglobal.yale.edu/content/can-china-and-turkey-forge-new-silk-road. Accessed on 8 September 2016.

Kenya Airports Authority. Nairobi – Jomo Kenyatta International Airport-NBO. http://www.kaa.go.ke/airports/nairobi-jomo-kenyatta-intl-airport

Kielstra, Paul. *The New Silk Road: Afro-Eurasian investment*. Global Financial Institute Deutsche Bank, November 2014.

Kim, Se-jeong. S. Korea revives ancient Silk Road, in: *People*, 23.09.2008. http://www.koreatimes.co.kr/www/news/people/2016/05/178_31538. html

King, Mike. DB Schenker launches eastbound Europe-China rail option, in: *Lloyd's Loading List*. http://www.lloydsloadinglist.com/freight-directory/ rail/DB-Schenker-launches-eastbound-Europe-China-rail-option/1682. htm#.Vz2UqCFO10Q

Kolej Transsyberyjska. Jekaterynburg. http://www.kolejtranssyberyjska.pl/ stacja-jekaterynburg

Korybko, Andrew. The Silk Road stretches to South America, in: *Oriental Review*, 20.05.2015. http://orientalreview.org/2015/05/20/the-silk-road-stretches-to-south-america/

Kosolapova, Elena. Kazakhstan-China pipeline starts operating at full capacity, in: *trend news agency*, 1.12.2015. http://en.trend.az/business/energy/2462953.html

Kouros, Alexis. The New Silk Road, in: *Helsinki Times*, 10.11.2015. http://www.helsinkitimes.fi/world-int/world-news/international-news/13608-the-new-silk-road.html

Koutantou, Angeliki & Goh, Brenda. After Piraeus Port, China's COSCO eyes Greek trains to build Europe hub – sources, in: *Reuters*, 5.02.2016. http://www.reuters.com/article/greece-china-port-idUSL8N14X17R

Kozak, Michał. Ukraine joints the Silk Road, in: *Central European Financial Observer*, 16.02.2016. http://www.financialobserver.eu/cse-and-cis/ukraine/ukraine-joins-the-silk-road/

Kratz, Agatha. China's AIIB: A triumph in public diplomacy, in: *China Analysis*, June 2015.

Kucera, Joshua. The New Silk Road?, in: *The Diplomat*, 11.11.2011. http://thediplomat.com/2011/11/the-new-silk-road/

Kucera, Joshua. U.S.: We're for The New Silk Road – If It Bypasses Iran, in: *EurAsiaNet*, 29.03.2012. http://www.eurasianet.org/node/65200

Kundu, Shohini. The New Silk Road: For the riches or the wretches?, in: *The Huffington Post*, 30.06.2015. http://www.huffingtonpost.com/shohini-kundu/the-new-silk-road-for-the_b_7692688.html

Kyle, Wang. Chengdu, in: China-Britain Business Council, http://www.cbbc.org/about-us/other/cbbc-cities/cbbc-city-chengdu/

Kunge, James. How the Silk Road plans will be financed, in: Financial Times, 9.05.2016. https://www.ft.com/content/e83ced94-0bd8-11e6-9456-444ab5211a2f. Accessed on 12 January 2017.

Kuriakose, Joy. Project 'Mausam'- Mausam/Mawsim. http://ignca.nic.in/mausam.htm

La Gaceta. Dario Oficial. no 16, Managua, Acuerdo Marco de Concesión e Implementación con Relación a El Canal de Nicaragua y Proyectos de Desarro. http://legislacion.asamblea.gob.ni/SILEG/Gacetas.nsf/0/f1ecd8f640b8e6ce06257b8f005bae22/$FILE/Ley%20No.%20840.%20Contrato%20en%20ingl%C3%A9s.pdf

Lee, Brianna. China, Brazil, Peru Eye Transcontinental Railway Megaproject, in: International Business Times, 5.19.2015. http://www.ibtimes.com/china-brazil-peru-eye-transcontinental-railway-megaproject-1930003

Lee, Eddie. Hong Kong businesses warm to New Silk Road initiatives, in: South China Morning Post, 20.04.2015. http://www.scmp.com/news/hong-kong/economy/article/1771641/hong-kong-businesses-warm-new-silk-road-initiatives

Lee, Victor Robert. China Builds Space-Monitoring Base in the Americas, in: *The Diplomat*, 24.05.2016. http://thediplomat.com/2016/05/china-builds-space-monitoring-base-in-the-americas/. Accessed on 9 September 2016.

Leer, Yeroen van der & Yau, Joshua. China's new silk route. The long and winding road, in: PWC's Growth Market Centre, February 2016.

Levchenko, Anastasia. Kenya to reap rewards as trade hub in China's One Belt, One Road Initiative, in: Sputnik News, 16.12.2015. http://sputniknews.com/business/20151216/1031859601/kenya-china-trade.html

Levin, Dan. Silk Road market caters to lovers of acceleration, handling and plumage, in: The New York Times, 15.02.2016. http://www.nytimes.com/2016/02/16/world/asia/china-xinjiang-uighur-pigeons.html?_r=0

Li, Yu, Peng, Chao & Peng, Yining.; Chengdu attractive to international businesses, in: China Daily, 10.03.2015. http://www.chinadaily.com.cn/china/2015-03/10/content_19765330.htm

Lin, Christiana. The New Silk Road, in: *Policy Focus*, April 2011. The Washington Institute for Near East Policy.

Lin, Justin Yifu. Industry transfer to Africa good for all, in: *China Daily*, 20.01.2015. http://usa.chinadaily.com.cn/epaper/2015-01/20/content_19357725.htm

Lin, Justin Yifu, China's Silk Road Vision, in: *Project Sindicate*, 21.01.2016. https://www.project-syndicate.org/onpoint/china-maritime-silk-road-economic-belt-by-justin-yifu-lin-2016-01?barrier=true

Liu, Jing. The ancient city takes a new route along the Silk Road, in: *China Daily*, 18.09.2015. http://www.chinadaily.com.cn/china/60thxjannivesary/2015-09/18/content_21911982.htm

Liu, Yunshan. Hold High the Banner of Advanced Culture, in: *Renmin Ribao*, 11.12.2002.

Lolos, Marios. Spotlight: COSCO's acquisition of Greek Piraeus Port to further contribute to local economy, in: *Xinhuanet*, 8.04.2016. http://news.xinhuanet.com/english/2016-04/09/c_135263687.htm

Ma, Junjie. The New Silk Road and the power of ideas, in: *The Diplomat*, 10.02.2015. http://thediplomat.com/2015/02/the-new-silk-road-and-the-power-of-ideas/

Maasdorp, Leslie. What is 'new' about the New Development Bank?, in: *World Economic Forum*, 26.10.2015. https://www.weforum.org/agen da/2015/08/what-is-new-about-the-new-development-bank/. Accesssed on 12 January 2017.

Macau Hub. China construction hyway delivers Moçâmedes railway reconstruction project in Angola, 14.09.2015. http://www.macauhub.com.mo/en/2015/09/14/china-construction-hyway-delivers-mocamedes-railway-reconstruction-project-in-angola/. Accesssed on 09.09.2016

MacDowall, Andrew. China looks to Europe – through the Balkans, in: Financial Times. Blogs, 19.12.2014. http://blogs.ft.com/beyond-brics/2014/12/19/china-looks-to-europe-through-the-balkans/

Mackinder, Halford John. The geographical pivot of history, in: *The Geographical Society*, vol. 23, no 4, 1904, 421–444.

Maersk. http://www.maersk.com/en

Magnuszewska, Agnieszka. W kwietniu odjedzie pierwszy towarowy pociąg z Łodzi do chińskiego Chengdu, in: *Nasze Miasto*, 28.03.2014. http://lodz.naszemiasto.pl/artykul/w-kwietniu-odjedzie-pierwszy-towarowy-pociag-z-lodzi-do,2214686,art,t,id,tm.html

Magnuszewska, Agnieszka. Pociągi Chengdu – Łódź. Z Chin przyjechało już 30 tys. ton towarów, in: *Dziennik Łódzki*, 22.12.2014. http://www.dzienniklodzki.pl/artykul/3692610,pociagi-chengdu-lodz-z-chin-przyjechalo-juz-30-tys-ton-towarow,id,t.html

Magnuszewska, Agnieszka. Łódź – Chiny. Pociągi cargo do Chengdu z towarami z regionu, in: *Nasze Miasto*, 19.08.2015. http://lodz.nasze miasto.pl/artykul/lodz-China-pociagi-cargo-do-chengdu-z-towarami-z-regionu,3483522,art,t,id,tm.html

Makinen, Julie. Violet Law: China's bold gambit to cement trade with Europe – along the ancient Silk Road, in: *Los Angeles Times*, 01.05.2016. http://www.latimes.com/world/asia/la-fg-china-silk-road-20160501-story.html

Mertens, Matthias. Along the New Silk Road, 01.04.2016. https://newold silkroad.wordpress.com/2016/04/01/xiamen/

Meyer, Eric. With oil and gas pipelines, China takes a shortcut through Myanmar, in: *Forbes*, 9.02.2015. http://www.forbes.com/sites/ericrmey er/2015/02/09/oil-and-gas-china-takes-a-shortcut/#2bc303e22d40. Accesssed on 11 October 2016.

Mining Technology, Aktogay Copper Mine. http://www.mining-technolo gy.com/projects/aktogay-copper-mine/. Accesssed on 6 December 2016.

Ministry of Foreign Affairs of the People's Republic of China. President Xi Jinping delivers important speech and proposes to build a Silk Road economic belt with Central Asian Countries, 7.09.2013. http://www. fmprc.gov.cn/mfa_eng/topics_665678/xjpfwzysiesgjtfhshzzfh_665686/ t1076334.shtml

Ministry of Foreign Affairs of the People's Republic of China. Foreign Minister Wang Yi answers journalists' question on China's diplomacy, in: *Foreign Policy and Foreign Relations*, 8.03.2015. qtd. in Bondaz, Antoine. Rebalancing.

Mission of the People's Republic of China to the UN. The Silk Road – From past to the future, 4.03.2014. http://www.china-un.org/eng/gyzg/ t1134206.htm

Molavi, Afshin. Five ways the 'new Silk Road' could transform the global economy, in: *Credit Suisse*, 27.11.2015. https://www.credit-suisse.com/ us/en/articles/articles/news-and-expertise/2015/11/en/five-ways-the-new-silk-road-could-transform-the-global-economy.html

Morgan Philips. Aviation "new silk road" set to become a leader for Gulf growth. 17.11.2015. http://www.morganphilipsexecutivesearch.com/ blog/aviation-new-silk-road-set-to-become-a-leader-for-gulf-growth/

Moritz, Rudolf. One Belt, One Road: The Silk Road, in: *Mercator Institute for China Studies*, December 2015. http://www.merics.org/en/merics-analysis/infographicchina-mapping/china-mapping.html

Moss, Chris. Silk Road: Trip of a lifetime, in: The Telegraph, 01.09.2014. http://www.telegraph.co.uk/travel/destinations/asia/articles/Silk-Road-Trip-of-a-Lifetime/

Możdżyński, Bogdan. Chiński sen Tomasza Grzelaka, in: *Forbes*, 23.03.2016. http://www.forbes.pl/chinski-sen-tomasza-grzelaka,artykuly,202996,1,1. html#

Municipalidad Provincial De Ilo. http://www.mpi.gob.pe/

Na kolei. Nowy Bursztynowy Szlak, 12.11.2015. http://www.nakolei.pl/com ponent/k2/item/5642-nowy-bursztynowy-szlak. Accesssed on 11 November 2016.

National Development and Reform Commission People's Republic of China. http://en.ndrc.gov.cn/

National Development and Reform Commission People's Republic of China. Vision and Actions on Jointly Building Silk Road Economic Belt and 21st-Century Maritime Silk Road, 28.03.2015. http://en.ndrc.gov.cn/ newsrelease/201503/t20150330_669367.html

Nazemroaya, Mahdi Darius, Neither greater Asia nor greater Europe: America's "chaos" versus a Silk World Order, in: *Strategic Culture Foundation Online Journal.* http://www.strategic-culture.org/news/2015/07/03/neither-greater-asia-nor-greater-europe-america-chaos-versus-silk-world-order.html

Nazemroaya, Mahdi Darius. The Silk World Order, in: *Modern Diplomacy,* 14.07.2015. http://moderndiplomacy.eu/index.php?option=com_ k2&view=item&id=847:the-silk-world-order&Itemid=490

New China. "One Belt One Road" initiative achieves series of important early-stage harvest, 22.05.2016. http://news.xinhuanet.com/english/2016-05/ 22/c_135379044.htm

New Development Bank. About us. https://www.ndb.int/about-us/essence/ history/. Accesssed on 23 April 2018.

New Silk Roads. http://www.newsilkroads.org/

New Silk Road Company Ltd. https://www.difc.ae/public-register/new-silk-road-company-ltd

New Silk Road Group. http://www.hktdc.com/manufacturers-suppliers/ New-Silk-Road-Group-Ltd/en/1X052D5S/

New Silk Road Institute Prague. http://nsrip.org/cs/. Accesssed on 21 December 2016.

New Silk Road Investment. http://www.nsr.com.sg/html/home.html

News of The Communist Party of China. http://english.cpc.people.com.cn/

Ni, Peimin. The underlying philosophy and impact of the New Silk Road World Order, in: *WPD Dialogue of Civilizations,* 16.10.2015. http:// www.wpfdc.org/blog/politics/19534-the-underlying-philosophy-and-impact-of-the-new-silk-road-world-order

Nogaj, Wioletta. Kolejny śmiały chiński projekt, in: *Co słychać w biznesie*, 24.05.2015. http://www.coslychacwbiznesie.pl/biznes/kolejny-smialy-chinski-projekt

Noori, Lailuma; New transit routes pave way for trade, in: The Kabul Times, 05.06.2016. http://thekabultimes.gov.af/index.php/opinions/politics/10790-new-transit-routes-pave-way-for-trade.html

Nuttall, Clare. Building the new Silk Road, in: *Khorgos*, December 2012. http://www.mcps-khorgos.kz/en/smi-review/building-new-silk-road

Nye, Joseph S. The rise of China's soft power, in: The Wall Street Journal, 29.12.2005.

Pannier, Bruce. How far will China go in Central Asia?, in: *Radio Free Europe*, 08.06.2015. http://www.rferl.org/content/qishloq-ovozi-chinese-influence-growing-roundtable/27060377.html

Parke, Phoebe. Kenya's $13 billion railway project is taking shape, in: CNN, 16.05.2016. http://edition.cnn.com/2016/05/15/africa/kenya-railway-east-africa/

Partridge, Ben. Georgia: Shevardnadze to host Silk Road Conference, in: *Radio Free Europe*, 09.06.1998. http://www.rferl.org/content/article/1088808.html

Patton, Dominique. Xinjiang cotton at crossroads of China's new Silk Road, in: *Reuters*, 11.01.2016. http://www.reuters.com/article/us-china-xinjiang-cotton-insight-idUSKCN0UQ00320160112

People.cn. Xinjiang's Koktokay National Geopark in most beautiful season, 10.05.2013. http://en.people.cn/205040/8239497.html

People's Daily. Of the new Silk Road. http://en.people.cn/102775/310175/310176/index.html

Peyrouse, Sebastien. Building a New Silk Road? Central Asia in the New World Order, in: *Origins*, http://origins.osu.edu/article/building-new-silk-road-central-asia-new-world-order

Phillips, Tom. Brazil's huge new port highlights China's drive into South America, in: The Guardian, 15.09.2010. http://www.theguardian.com/world/2010/sep/15/brazil-port-china-drive

Pillalamarri, Akhilesh. Project Mausam: India's answer to China's 'Maritime Silk Road', in: *The Diplomat*, 18.09.2014. http://thediplomat.com/2014/09/project-mausam-indias-answer-to-chinas-maritime-silk-road/

Pinto, Anet Josline & Thomas, Denny. Freeport to sell prized Tenke copper mine to China Moly for $2.65 billion, in: *Reuters*, 09.05.2016., http://www.reuters.com/article/us-freeport-mcmoran-tenke-cmoc-idUSKCN0Y015U. Accesssed on 12 January 2017.

Piraeus Container Terminal SA. http://www.pct.com.gr/

Plácido Dos Santos, Gustavo. The United Arab Emirates, Africa and Angola in the New Silk Road – Analysis, in: *Eurasia Review*, 03.07.2015. http://www.eurasiareview.com/03072015-the-united-arab-emirates-africa-and-angola-in-new-silk-road-analysis/. Accesssed on 17 January 2017.

Polskie Radio.pl. Jedwabny Szlak. Eksperci: Poland może na tym dobrze zarobić, 20.06.2016. http://www.polskieradio.pl/42/273/Artykul/1633785,Jedwabny-Szlak-Eksperci-Poland-moze-na-tym-dobrze-zarobic

Polyus, Natalka. http://polyus.com/en/operations/development_projects/natalka/. Accesssed on 6 December 2016.

Port of Hamburg. Gigantic 19,100-TEU containership CSCL GLOBE in Hamburg on maiden voyage – growth in China trade continues. https://www.hafen-hamburg.de/en/news/gigantic-19-100-teu-containership-cscl-globe-in-hamburg-on-maiden-voyage-growth-in-china-trade-continues---32634

Port of Hamburg. History. https://www.hafen-hamburg.de/en/history

Post, Colin. Las Bambas: Peru's largest copper mine starts production, in: *Peru Reports*, 18.01.2016. http://perureports.com/2016/01/18/las-bambas-perus-largest-copper-mine-starts-production/. Accesssed on 12 January 2017.

President of Russia. Treaty on Eurasian Economic Union signed, 29.05.2014. http://en.kremlin.ru/events/president/news/45787

Prigogine, Ilya & Stengers, Isabelle. *Order out of chaos: Man's new dialogue with nature.* New York 1984.

Puls, Thomas. China's New Silk Road: The European perspective, in: *IW.Köln. Wissenschafft Kompetenz*, 04.06.2015.

Putin, Władymir; Press statements following Russian-Chinese talks. http://en.kremlin.ru/events/president/transcripts/49433. Accesssed on 15 June 2017.

Putin, Władymir; U.N. General Assembly speech, in: *The Washington Post*, 28.09.2015. https://www.washingtonpost.com/news/worldviews/wp/2015/09/28/read-putins-u-n-general-assembly-speech/

Putz, Catherine. Why the Trans-Caspian Transport Route matters, in: *The Diplomat*, 11.02.2016. http://thediplomat.com/2016/02/why-the-trans-caspian-transport-route-matters/

Pyffel, Radosław. Nowy Jedwabny Szlak i Nowy Bursztynowy Szlak – kluczowe chińskie projekty dla Polski i Europy, in: *Kresy*. http://www.kresy.pl/wydarzenia,europa-poludniowa?zobacz/nowy-jedwabny-szlak-i-nowy-bursztynowy-szlak-kluczowe-chinskie-projekty-dla-polski-i-europy. Accesssed on 11 November 2016

QIC. The New Silk Road – Shifting the economic centre of the world east. http://www.qic.com.au/knowledge-centre/the-new-silk-road-20160301

Radio Warszawa. Polska ma być dla Chin mostem do Europy. 21.06.2016. http://radiowarszawa.com.pl/2016/06/Poland-i-China-wkraczaja-na-nowy-jedwabny-szlak/

Railway Gazette. Three presidents inaugurate rebuilt Benguela Railway, http://www.railwaygazette.com/news/infrastructure/single-view/view/three-presidents-inaugurate-rebuilt-benguela-railway.html. Accesssed on 9 September 2016.

Railway Gazette. China funds Argentina's rail revival, 10.07.2010. http://www.railwaygazette.com/news/policy/single-view/view/china-funds-argentinas-rail-revival.html. Accesssed on 09.09.2016

Railway Gazette. Iran – Turkmenistan – Kazakhstan rail link inaugurated, 04.12.2014. http://www.railwaygazette.com/news/news/asia/single-view/view/iran-turkmenistan-kazakhstan-rail-link-inaugurated.html

Railway Gazette. Marmaray tunnel opens to link Europe with Asia, 29.10.2013. http://www.railwaygazette.com/news/single-view/view/marmaray-tunnel-opens-to-link-europe-with-asia.html

Rakhmetova, Klara. Kazakhstan-China Oil Pipeline Project. http://www.energycharter.org/fileadmin/DocumentsMedia/Presentations/CBP-KZ-CN.pdf

Rana, Pradumna B. & Chia, Wai-Mun. The Revival of the Silk Roads (Land Connectivity) in Asia. RSIS Working Paper, no 274, 12.05.2014. http://www.rsis.edu.sg/wp-content/uploads/2014/07/WP274.pdf. Accesssed on 11 October 2016.

Raza, Syed Irfan. China given contract to operate Gwadar port, in: *Dawn*, 18.08.2013. http://www.dawn.com/news/786992/china-given-contract-to-operate-gwadar-port

Redcat. Kyong Park: New Silk Roads, 02.03.2010. http://www.redcat.org/event/kyong-park

Rehn, Cecilia. Kazakhstan-China oil pipeline could start operating at its full capacity by 2014, in: *Energy Global World Pipelines*, 09.11.2012. http://www.energyglobal.com/pipelines/business-news/09112012/Ka zakhstan_to_China_oil_pipeline_could_start_operating_at_its_full_ca pacity_by_2014/

Reyaz M. TAPI pipeline: A new silk route or a pipe dream? in: *Aljazeera*, 10.12.2015. http://www.aljazeera.com/news/2015/12/tapi-pipeline-silk-route-pipe-dream-151215211343976.html

RFC5 Baltic-Adriatic Corridor. http://rfc5.eu/. Accesssed on 11 November 2016.

Rolland, Nadège. China's New Silk Road, in: *The National Bureau of Asian Research*. http://nbr.org/research/activity.aspx?id=531

Rubin, Barnett. The TAPI Pipeline and paths to peace in Afghanistan, in: *The New Yorker*, 30.12.2015. http://www.newyorker.com/news/news-desk/the-tapi-pipeline-and-paths-to-peace-in-afghanistan

Rukhadze, Vasili, Completion of Baku–Tbilisi–Kars Railway Project Postponed Again, in: *Global Research and Analysis*, 02.03.2016. http://www.jamestown.org/single/?tx_ttnews[tt_news]=45159&no_cache=1#.V0r VOiFO10Q

Rupak, Bhattacharjee. The emerging Bangladesh China India Myanmar-Economic Corridor and its opportunities, in: *The Eastern Today*, 11.02.2016. http://www.eastern-today.com/entries/editorial/the-emerg ing-bangladesh-china-india-myanmar-economic-corridor-and-its-oppor tunities

RussiaPl.Info. Kolej transsyberyjska, 17.09.2014. http://www.Russiapl. info/podroze/rosyjskie-miasta-i-regiony/kolej-transsyberyjska.html

Rutz, Julia. First test train passes the Trans-Caspian International Transport Route, in: *The Astana Times*, 09.02.2016. http://astanatimes. com/2016/02/first-test-train-passes-the-trans-caspian-international-transport-route/

SACE Foundation. http://www.sacefoundation.org/contact-us/

Salehi, Zarghona. Ghani, Aliyev confer on gas pipeline project, in: *Pajhwok Afghan News*, 02.12.2014. http://www.elections.pajhwok.com/en/2014/12/02/ghani-aliyev-confer-gas-pipeline-project

Salvacion, Manny. Maersk keen on working with Chinese firms in overseas investments, in: *Yibada*, 11.11.2015. http://en.yibada.com/articles/83950/20151111/maersk-keen-working-chinese-firms-overseas-investments.htm

Sant, Shannon van. Hong Kong looks to key role in China's New Silk Road, in: *Voice of America*, 11.03.2016. http://www.voanews.com/content/hong-kong-looks-to-key-role-in-china-new-silk-road/3231613.html

Saudi Press Agency. Tanker from Ras Tanura brings Arabian crude for Qingdao Refinery, 14.06.2008. http://spa.gov.sa/564968

Sawer. East wind train blows in from China to re-open Silk Road trail, in: The Telegraph, 18.01.2017. http://www.telegraph.co.uk/news/2017/01/18/east-wind-train-blows-china-re-open-silk-road-trail/. Accesssed on 18 January 2017.

Schaefer, Michael. Co-driving the New Silk Road, in: *Berlin Policy Journal*, 12.01.2016. http://berlinpolicyjournal.com/co-driving-the-new-silk-road/

Sen, Tansen. The Travel Records of Chinese Pilgrims Fazian, Xuanzang, and Yijing. http://afe.easia.columbia.edu/special/travel_records.pdf

Serbia Construction. Chinese to build new Belgrade bridge. http://www.serbiaconstruction.com/content/chinese-to-build-new-belgrade-bridge/

Shadi, Khan Saif. Afghanistan eyes alternate routes for global trade, in: *AA*, 03.01.2015. http://aa.com.tr/en/economy/afghanistan-eyes-alternate-routes-for-global-trade/87452

Shanghai Academy of Social Sciences. Professor Ni Peimin was invited to deliver a lecture at New Think Tank Forum, 19.01.2016. http://english.sass.org.cn:8001/lecture/1723.jhtml

Shanghai Cooperation Organization. http://infoshos.ru/en/

Shanghai International Port. http://www.portshanghai.com.cn/en/channel1/channel11.html

Shenkar, Oded. *The Chinese century: The rising Chinese economy and its impact on the global economy, the balance of power, and your job.* Philadelphia 2007.

Shepard, Wade. An Inside Look At The New Crossroads Of Eurasia: Azerbaijan's New Port of Baku. https://www.forbes.com/sites/wadeshepard/2016/11/03/an-inside-look-at-the-new-crossroads-of-eurasia-azerbaijans-new-port-of-baku/#3abb36d553a4. Accesssed on 22 June 2017.

Shepard, Wade. Why The China-Europe "Silk Road" Rail Network is growing fast, in: *Forbes*, 28.01.2016. http://www.forbes.com/sites/wadeshepard/2016/01/28/why-china-europe-silk-road-rail-transport-is-growing-fast/#3647515b7f24

Sherazi, Syed Zubair. Development of Gwadar port: Apprehensions of the locals. http://www.intermedia.org.pk/pdf/pak_afghan/Gwadar-Aug.pdf

Shi, Yinhong. The roles China ought to play in the world, in: *China US Focus*, 05.08.2012. http://www.chinausfocus.com/foreign-policy/the-role-china-ought-to-play-in-the-world/

Shirinov, Rashid. Azerbaijan, Kazakhstan, Georgia seeks to boost Trans-Caspian Int'l Route, in: *Azernews*, 17.05.2016. http://www.azernews.az/business/96716.html

Sil, Saumya. Is Iran's Chabahar port important to India?, in: *Quora*. https://www.quora.com/Is-Irans-Chabahar-port-important-to-India

Silk Road Film Festival. http://silkroadfilmfestival.com/the-festival/

Silk Road Foundation (Korea). http://www.silkroad-foundation.org/

Silk Road Foundation (USA). http://www.silkroadfoundation.org/toc/index.html

Silk Road Fund. http://www.silkroadfund.com.cn/enweb/23773/index.html. Accesssed on 17 June 2017.

Silk Road Group. http://silkroadgroup.net/silk-road-group/about/

Silk Road Group. Transportation. http://silkroadgroup.net/businesses/transportation/

Silk Road International Travel. http://www.silkroadtravel.gr/about/

Silk Road Railway. http://www.sundownersoverland.com/admin/traveldocs/categorised/304934.pdf

Silk Road Reporters. http://www.silkroadreporters.com/

Silk Road Treasure Tours. http://www.silkroadtreasuretours.com/

Silk Route Rail. http://www.silkrouterail.com/about-us.html

Simply Decoded. Project 'Mausam' by Ministry of Culture, 22.06.2014. http://www.simplydecoded.com/2014/06/22/project-mausam-ministry-culture/

Slobodchuk, Sergey. New Silk Road: Cherished dream or real transport corridor for Ukraine?, in: *EurAsia Daily*, 3.02.2016. https://eadaily.com/en/news/2016/02/03/new-silk-road-cherished-dream-or-real-transport-corridor-for-ukraine

Sprengel, Mieczysław & Sprengel, Katarzyna. *Evaluation of China's potential to become 21st century global power*. in: Prace Naukowe Akademii im. Jana Długosza w Częstochowie, vol. VI, 2014, 87–94.

Sputnik. Historic moment: Part of New Silk Road From China to Iran is Complete, 16.02.2016. http://sputniknews.com/business/20160216/1034868058/iran-china-silk-road.html

Stahl, Alan. *Zecca: The mint of Venice in the Middle Ages*. New York 2000.

Stamouli, Nektaria. Greece signs deal to sell stake in Port of Piraeus to China's Cosco, in: *The Wall Street Journal*, 8.04.2016. http://www.wsj.com/articles/greece-signs-deal-to-sell-stake-in-port-of-piraeus-to-chinas-cosco-1460130394

Starr, Frederick S. & Cornell, Svante E. (Eds.). Putin's grand strategy: The Eurasian Union and its discontents. The Central Asia-Caucasus Institute, 2014. http://www.silkroadstudies.org/resources/1409GrandStrategy.pdf

Summers, Tim. What exactly is 'one belt, one road'?, in: *The World Today*, vol. 71, no 5, 2015. https://www.chathamhouse.org/publication/twt/what-exactly-one-belt-one-road

Sundowners Overland. Sharing Asia overland. Differently. http://www.sundownersoverland.com/

Szafarz, Sylwester. Stare i nowe Jedwabne Szlaki, in: *CRI*, 7.01.2016. http://polish.cri.cn/1380/2016/01/07/341s134271.htm

Szczudlik-Tatar, Justyna. China's New Silk Road diplomacy, in: *Policy Paper*, no 34, 2013, 1–8.

Talmiz, Ahmad. Who's afraid of One Belt One Road?, in: *The Wire*, 3.06.2016. http://thewire.in/40388/one-belt-one-road-shaping-connectivities-and-politics-in-the-21st-century/

Tharoor, Ishaan. The world's longest train journey now begins in China, in: The Washington Post, 21.11.2014. https://www.washingtonpost.com/

news/worldviews/wp/2014/11/21/map-the-worlds-longest-train-journey-now-begins-in-china/

The Danish Chamber of Commerce. Hong Kong: Promotion of New Opportunities In Guangzhou Under "One Belt, One Road" and Free Trade Zone Strategy, 29.07.2015. http://www.dcc.hk/events/promotion-on-new-opportunities-in-guangzhou-under-one-belt-one-road-and-free-trade-zone-strategy/

The Dubai Mall. http://www.thedubaimall.com/en/

The Economic Times. 55 cities from 17 nations to take part in Silk Road Forum in China, 13.07.2015. http://articles.economictimes.indiatimes.com/2015-07-13/news/64370831_1_silk-road-economic-belt-urumqi-xinjiang

The Economist. Rulers of the new silk road, 03.06.2010. http://www.econo mist.com/node/16271573

The Hans India. What is Project Mausam?, 14.03.2016. http://www.the hansindia.com/posts/index/News-Analysis/2016-03-14/What-is-Project-Mausam/213413

The Hans India. Ashgabat Agreement, 24.03.2016. http://www.thehansin dia.com/posts/index/Hans-Classroom/2016-03-24/Ashgabat-Agree ment/215932

The International Dunhuang Project. The Silk Road Online. http://idp. bl.uk/

The International Schiller Institute. Build the World Land-Bridge!. http:// newparadigm.schillerinstitute.com/our-campaign/build-the-world-land-bridge/

The Kabul Times. Azure route a proper transit way to develop trade: Nasrat, 26.11.2014. http://thekabultimes.gov.af/index.php/newsnational/4764-azure-route-a-proper-transit-way-to-develop-trade-nasrat.html

The Maritime Executive. China eyes Kenyan Ports, 07.10.2015. http:// www.maritime-executive.com/article/china-eyeing-kenyan-ports

The Mirror. Bigger than the shard: Watch the world's largest container ship dock in the UK, 07.01.2015. http://www.mirror.co.uk/news/uk-news/bigger-shard-watch-worlds-largest-4937045

The National Council for Tourism and Antiquities. Archaeological sites. http://ncta.gov.ae/web/guest/archaeological-sites

The National People's Congress. http://www.npc.gov.cn/englishnpc/Organi zation/node_2846.htm

The Siberian Times. Major deal signed with China to explore gold deposits, 15.05.2015. http://siberiantimes.com/business/investment/news/n0217-major-deal-signed-with-china-to-explore-gold-deposits/. Accesssed on 6 December 2016.

The Silk Road, vol. 13, 2015. http://www.silkroadfoundation.org/newslet ter/vol13/srjournal_v13.pdf

The Silk Road International Arts Festival. http://www.silkroadart.net/en/ index.aspx

The Suez Canal Authority. http://www.suezcanal.gov.eg/

The Voice of Russia. Russian, Kazakh, Belarusian leaders sign treaty on creation of Eurasian Economic Union. 29.05.2014. http://sputniknews. com/voiceofrussia/news/2014_05_29/Russian-Kazakh-Belarusian-lead ers-sign-treaty-on-creation-of-Eurasian-Economic-Union-8877/

The World Land Bridge. https://larouchepac.com/world-landbridge

Tian, Xuefei. All aboard as freight trains revive Silk Road glory, in: The Telegraph, 17.07.2015. http://www.telegraph.co.uk/sponsored/china-watch/business/11732204/freight-trains-revive-silk-road-glory.html

Tiezzi, Shannon. China's 'New Silk Road' vision revealed, in: The Diplo mat, 09.05.2014. http://thediplomat.com/2014/05/chinas-new-silk-road-vision-revealed/

Tomlinson, Simon. China builds first overseas military base near Ethiopia for ships, helicopters and special forces in quest to become naval superpow er, in: The Sun, 22.08.2016. https://www.thesun.co.uk/news/1652050/ djibouti-china-builds-first-overseas-military-base-in-dijbouti-for-ships-helicopters-and-special-forces-in-bid-to-become-naval-superpower. Ac cesssed on 6 December 2016.

Topham, Gwyn. Emirates' concourse for A380s is another staging post on new Silk Road, in: The Guardian, 03.03.2013. https://www.theguard ian.com/business/2013/mar/03/emirates-new-concourse-dubai-silk-road

TRACECA. http://www.traceca-org.org/en/home/

Trans-Siberian Travel. http://www.transsib.com/trans-siberian-train-tickets-prices.html

Travel China Guide. Guangdong Maritime Silk Road Museum. https://www.travelchinaguide.com/cityguides/guangdong/yangjiang/maritime-silk-road-museum.htm

Travel China Guide. Southern Silk Road. https://www.travelchinaguide.com/silk-road/southern-route.htm

Trusewicz, Iwona. Prąd z Azji centralnej zasili Pakistan, in: *Rzeczpospolita*, 19.05.2016. http://www.rp.pl/Energianews/305199936-Prad-z-Azji-Centralnej-zasili-Pakistan.html

Turebekova, Aiman. Kazakhstan supports New Silk Road and One Belt, One Road Initiatives, Official Says, in: The Astana Times, 05.05.2016. http://astanatimes.com/2016/05/kazakhstan-supports-new-silk-road-and-one-belt-one-road-initiatives-official-says/

Turksoy. The Conference entitled "The International Silk Road Congress: Rethinking the Road of Trade, Cooperation and Peace" took place in Istanbul. 31.10.2013. http://www.turksoy.org/en/news/2013/10/31/the_international_silk_road_congress_rethinking_the_ticaret_isbirligi_ve_baris_havzasini_

UAE Interact. New archaeological discovery confirms the long history of UAE civilization in West Abu Dhabi, 2.03.2009. http://www.uaeinteract.com/docs/New_archaeological_discovery_confirms_the_long_history_of_UAE_civilization_in_West_Abu_Dhabi/34558.htmUNCTAD; http://unctad.org/en/Pages/aboutus.aspx

UNCTAD. Investment Guide to the Silk Road. United Nations 2014. http://unctad.org/en/PublicationsLibrary/diae2014d3_en.pdf. Accesssed on 12 October 2016.

UNESCO. The city of Herat. http://whc.unesco.org/en/tentativelists/1927/

UNESCO. Maritime Silk Road Museum of GUANGDONG. http://en.unesco.org/silkroad/silk-road-institutions/maritime-silk-road-museum-guangdong

UNESCO. Reviving the Historic Silk Roads: UNESCO's new Online Platform. http://www.unesco.org/new/en/culture/themes/dialogue/routes-of-dialogue/silk-road/

UNESCO. The UNESCO Silk Road online platform. https://en.unesco.org/silkroad/unesco-silk-road-online-platform

UNESCO. Xi'an. http://en.unesco.org/silkroad/content/xian

UNESCO Silk Road. Herat. http://en.unesco.org/silkroad/content/herat

UNESCO Silk Road. Turkey. http://en.unesco.org/silkroad/countries-along side-silk-road-routes/turkey

U.S. Department of State. New Silk Road Ministerial. http://www.state.gov/r/pa/prs/ps/2011/09/173765.htm

Uzbekistan Today. Tashkent SCO summit to be held on June 23–24, 01.07.2016. http://www.ut.uz/en/politics/tashkent_sco_summit_to_be_held_on_june_2324

Valantin, Jean-Michel. Turkey: An energy and environmental power, in: The Read (Team) Analysis Society, 23.02.2015. https://www.redanalysis.org/2015/02/23/turkey-russia-china-creating-new-energy-environmental-power/. Accesssed on 8 September 2016.

Vandenberg, Paul & Kikkawe, Khan. Global value chains, in: *Policy Brief*, no 2, May 2015, http://www.adb.org/sites/default/files/publication/160572/adbi-pb2015-2.pdf

Wang, Huning. Culture as national soft power, in: *Journal of Fudan University*, March 1993.

Wang, Yiwei; How to deal with geopolitical risks during the implementation of the One Belt One Road, in: *Gongshi wang*, 29.04.2015.

Watts, Jonathan. Argentina leader leaves controversial legacy with Patagonia dams project, in: The *Guardian*, 1.12.2015. https://www.theguardian.com/world/2015/dec/01/argentina-president-cristina-fernandez-de-kirchner-patagonia-hydroelectric-dam-project. Accesssed on 9 September 2016.

Waugh, Daniel C. The Silk Roads in history. http://penn.museum/documents/publications/expedition/PDFs/52-3/waugh.pdf

Waugh, Daniel C. Richthofen's "Silk Roads": Toward the archaeology of a concept, in: *The Silk Road*, vol. 5, no 1, 2007,1-8.

Wen, Jiabao. Our historical tasks at the primary stage of socialism and several issues concerning China's foreign policy, in: *Renmin Ribao*, 07.03.2007.

Wheeler, Andre. The New China Silk Road (One Belt, One Road): Myanmar's influence and potential benefits, 04.01.2016. https://www.linkedin.com/pulse/new-china-silk-road-one-belt-myanmars-influence-benefits-wheeler

Wiadomości. Chiny: Bronisław Komorowski gościem partii komunistycznej. http://wiadomosci.onet.pl/swiat/China-bronislaw-komorowskigosciem-partii-komunistycznej/f04b2w. Accessed on 15 October 2016.

Winnicki, Piotr. Nowy Jedwabny Szlak. Droga do budowy imperium, in: *BiznesPL*, 15.10.2015. http://biznes.pl/magazyny/handel/nowy-jedwabny-szlak-droga-do-budowy-imperium/cct76t

Winter, Tim. One Belt, One Road, one heritage: Cultural diplomacy and the Silk Road, in: *The Diplomat*, 29.03.2016. http://thediplomat.com/2016/03/one-belt-one-road-one-heritage-cultural-diplomacy-and-the-silk-road/

Wollmer, Göran. The Modern Silk Road. http://schenkeronline.dk/download/CBS_Summit_2015/TheNewSilkRoad_GoranWollmer_SCM_Summit2015.pdf

Wong, Alfred. China's Telecommunications Boom in Africa: Causes and Consequences, E-International Relations, 21.09.2015. http://www.e-ir.info/2015/09/21/chinas-telecommunications-boom-in-africa-causes-and-consequences/. Accesssed on 17 January 2017.

Wong, John. China's rising economic soft power, 25.03.2016. http://blogs.nottingham.ac.uk/chinapolicyinstitute/2016/03/25/chinas-rising-economic-soft-power/

Wong, Tsoi-lai Catherine. Xi'an readies for key role in 'One Belt, One Road' initiative, in: The Global Times, 21.04.2015. http://www.globaltimes.cn/content/917943.shtml

World Port Source. Port of Xiamen. http://www.worldportsource.com/ports/commerce/CHN_Port_of_Xiamen_2510.php

Woźniak, Adam. Z Łódzkiego coraz bliżej do Chin, in: *Życie Ziemi Łódzkiej*, 31.05.2016. http://www.rp.pl/Zycie-Ziemi-Lodzkiej/305319839-Z-Lodzkiego-coraz-blizej-do-Chin.html

WPolityce.Pl. Premier Szydło: "Nowy Jedwabny Szlak to ogromne możliwości i korzyści gospodarcze. To nasza wspólna droga do rozwoju", 20.06.2016. http://wpolityce.pl/polityka/297460-premier-szydlo-nowy-jedwabny-szlak-to-ogromne-mozliwosci-i-korzysci-gospodarcze-to-nasza-wspolna-droga-do-rozwoju

Wright, Gilly. New Silk Road to expand China's trade financie renminbi rise, in: Global Finance, February 2016. https://www.gfmag.com/magazine/february-2016/new-silk-road-expand-chinas-trade-finance-renminbi-rise

Wu, Annie. Urumqi Grand Bazaar, in: *China Highlights*, 13.01.2015. http://www.chinahighlights.com/urumqi/attraction/urumqi-grand-bazaar.htm

Wu, Annie. Xinjiang Silk Road Museum, in: *China Highlights*, 13.01.2015. http://www.chinahighlights.com/urumqi/attraction/xinjiang-silk-road-museum.htm

Xi, Jinping. Promote Friendship Between Our People and Work Together to Build a Bright Future. http://www.fmprc.gov.cn/mfa_eng/wjdt_665385/zyjh_665391/t1078088.shtml. Accesssed on 22 June 2017.

Xi, Jinping. Silk Road Economic Belt. http://english.cntv.cn/program/china24/20130907/103428.shtml

Xi, Jinping. Speech at the the closing meeting of the first session of the 12th National People's Congress (NPC) at the Great Hall of the People in Beijing, capital of China, March 17, 2013, in: *Xinhuanet*, 17.03.2013. http://news.xinhuanet.com/english/china/2013-03/17/c_132239786.htm

Xi, Jinping. Speech at Nazarbayev University (video), 9.08.2013. http://english.cntv.cn/20130908/100822.shtml

Xi, Jinping. Speech by Chinese President Xi Jinping to Indonesian Parliament. http://www.asean-china-center.org/english/2013-10/03/c_133062675.htm

Xie, Jun. Yiwu-Europe railway can help boost trade even at low end, in: The Global Times, 24.06.2015. http://www.globaltimes.cn/content/928726.shtml

Xinhua. China sets up largest gold fund, 23.05.2015. http://news.xinhuanet.com/english/2015-05/23/c_134264324.htm. Accesssed on 15 December 2016.

Xinhua. Feature: Ukraine-China cargo train on Silk Road opens up prospects for trade, promotion, 1.02.2016. http://news.xinhuanet.com/english/2016-02/01/c_135062009.htm

Xinhua. Argentina-China dams project gains new momentum, 30.04.2016. http://news.xinhuanet.com/english/2016-04/30/c_135325462.htm. Accesssed on 9 September 2016.

Xinhuanet. Xi Jinping: Pursuing dream for 1.3 billion Chinese, 17.03.2013. http://news.xinhuanet.com/english/china/2013-03/17/c_124467411.htm

Xinhuanet. Xi's visit to Belarus highly praised, 13.05.2015. http://news.xinhuanet.com/english/2015-05/13/c_134235227.htm

Yazıcı, Hayati. Turkey-EU Relations and the Customs Union: Expectations versus the reality. http://turkishpolicy.com/Files/ArticlePDF/turkey-eu-relations-and-the-customs-union-expectations-versus-the-reality-spring-2012-en.pdf

Yiwu Market Guide. http://www.yiwu-market-guide.com/yiwu-internation al-trade-city.html

Zaborski, Andrzej (Ed. and Trans.). *Wspaniały świat Oceanu Indyjskiego Sulajmana Kupca*. Kraków, Księgarnia Akademicka 1998.

Zakaria, Fareed. *The Post-American World*. New York, W.W. Norton & Company 2008.

Zepp-LaRouche, Helga. The New Silk Road leads to the future of mankind!, https://worldlandbridge.com/introduction/

Zepp-LaRouche, Helga. The New Silk Road will change the world, in: *EIR*, 29.08.2014. http://www.larouchepub.com/hzl/2014/4134silk_rd_change_wrld.html

Zepp-LaRouche, Helga, Billington Michael & Douglas, Rachel (Eds.). *The New Silk Road becomes the World Land-Bridge*. Washington, EIR Washington 2014.

Zhang, Yesui. 'The One Belt, One Road' Initiative is not a geopolitical tool. Speech at China Development Forum, in: *Xinhua*, 21.03.2015.

Zhao, Minghao. China's new Silk Road initiative, in: *Istituto Affari Internazionali Working Papers*, no 15, 2015.

Zhen, Luo. One Belt One Road, in: *China Stocks*, 14.04.2015. http://www.chinastocks.net/cctv-unveils-map-of-the-new-silk-road/

Zhengzhou International Hub Development and Construction. 'One Belt One Road'. http://en.zzguojilugang.com/article.php?id=57

Zhong, Nan. COSCO launches world's largest oil tanker fleet, in: *China Daily*, 7.06.2016. http://www.chinadaily.com.cn/business/2016-06/07/content_25632170.htm

Zicheng, Ye. *Inside China's Grand Strategy: The Perspective from the People's Republic of China*. Lexington, University Press of Kentucky, 2010.

Азаттык. Торугарт бекетин жылдырууга ким уруксат берген?. http://www.azattyk.org/a/Kyrgyzstan_China_Border/1777779.html

БЕЛТА. Belarus ready to become 'western gate' for SCO, 24.06.2016. http://eng.belta.by/president/view/belarus-ready-to-become-western-gate-for-sco-92494-2016/

Цзи, Яньчи. Это новая модель глобального управления, in: Невское время, 12.06.2016. http://www.nvspb.ru/tops/eto-novaya-model-globalnogo-upravleniya-57593/?version=print

Кулинцев, Юрий. "Один пояс – один путь": инициатива с китайской спецификой, in: РСМД, 22.05.2015. http://russiancouncil.ru/blogs/riacexperts/?id_4=1868

Тавровский, Юрий. Новые мелодии "Шелкового пути", 16.07.2015. Russia. people.cn, http://russian.people.com.cn/n/2015/0716/c95181-8921285.html

Транссибирская магистраль. http://www.transsib.ru/

Қазақстан темір жолы. Seaport Aktau – reliable link of Kazakhstan's transit to foreign markets, 26.11.2015. http://www.railways.kz/en/node/9931

ҚазМұнайГаз. Kazakhstan-China oil Pipeline. http://www.kmg.kz/en/manu facturing/oil/kazakhstan_china/

Əliyeva, Aynur. Second container train on Trans-Caspian route reaches Georgia via Azerbaijan, in: *Report*, 3.10.2015. http://report.az/en/in frastructure/the-second-container-train-on-trans-caspian-international-transport-route-reaches-georgia-through-az/

Краткий путеводитель по Новому Шелковому Пути. Краткое изложение

Многие из нас слышали о Шелковом Пути. Уже несколько лет все чаще говорится о Новом Шелковом Пути. Этот краткий путеводитель предназначен для тех, кто хотел бы узнать больше об этом Новом Шелковом Пути.

А теперь приведем краткое изложение содержания этого путеводителя.

Новый Путь, также как и Старый – это сеть сообщений между разными, удаленными друг от друга местами.

Часть 1. – это пример выбранных сообщений и мест.

Часть 2. – это люди, учреждения и проекты.

Часть 3. – это значения и ценности, придаваемые Новому Пути разными людьми в разных местах.

Часть 4. – в ней говорится о том, чем Новый Путь является для мира, в котором мы живем, и его будущего.

Новый Путь и формируемый им Новый Шелковый Порядок Мира стоит рассматривать как взаимодействие, которое происходит между различными инициативами государств, фирм, организаций, людей. Иногда эти инициативы совпадают, соответствуют друг другу, а иногда расходятся или даже являются противоположными, как две фирмы или государства, каждое из которых стремится занять привилегированное положение. Некоторые инициативы связаны между собой, другие независимы. На самом деле, все происходящие между ними взаимодействия способствуют формированию Нового Пути и связанного с ним Нового Шелкового Мирового Порядка. Новый Путь представляет собой это взаимодействие, и в этом смысле можно говорить о многостороннем, многоаспектном и плюралистическом характере Нового Пути и Нового Порядка. Особую роль в строительстве Нового Пути и формировании связанного с ним Нового Порядка играет Китай, который устанавливает плюралистический, многокультурный мир. И здесь существует явный парадокс. Плюрализм Нового Пути и Нового Порядка, а также Великий Возрожденный Китай, выступающий за многокультурный мир, были бы тесно связаны друг с другом и взаимно способствовали бы своему развитию. (trans. Mirosław Bilowicki)

A Short Guide to the New Silk Road

Many of us have heard about the Silk Road. In recent years, however, a New Silk Road that has been on the lips of many. This short guide is addressed to all those who want to learn more about this New Road.

Now, a short guide to this short guide. The New Silk Road resembles the Old Road in that it represents an ensemble of relationships and connections among several distant places. Part 1 depicts some of these connections and places. Part 2 concerns people, institutions and projects. Part 3 deals with the various meanings and values attributed to the New Road by different people across the world. Part 4 explores what the New Silk Road means for the rest of the world, for the world we inhabit and for its future.

The New Road and the New World Order shaped by it can be viewed as a complex interaction of different initiatives proposed and/or undertaken by states, companies, organisations and individual people. These initiatives are sometimes convergent and congruent, but sometimes divergent or, even, conflicting, when companies or countries compete for influence, each striving to secure a privileged position for itself. Some of the initiatives are closely interconnected while other ones coexist independently. Yet, they all and, even more so, their interactions contribute to the formation of the New Road and its Silk New World Order. The New Road is this ceaseless interaction, and it is in this sense that we can speak of a multilateral, multipolar and pluralistic character of the New Road and the New Order. China, which postulates a pluralistic and multicultural world, is an essential agent in the building of the New Road and the New Order. This is where a genuine paradox lies. The pluralistic New Road (with its New Order) and the Great Reborn China advocating for a multicultural world would be interconnected and would thus mutually trigger each one's development.

Index of towns, ports and airports

INTERNATIONAL RELATIONS IN ASIA, AFRICA AND THE AMERICAS

Edited by Andrzej Mania & Marcin Grabowski

Band   1   Olga Barbasiewicz (ed.): Postwar Reconciliation in Central Europe and East Asia. 2018

Band   2   Adam Novis: A Short Guide to the New Silk Road. 2018

Band   3   Radka Havlová (ed.): Untangling the Mayhem: Crises and Prospects of the Middle East. 2018

www.peterlang.com